CHRIST, THE DIVINE NETWORK

Reflections on the Gospels for the A-cycle

Joseph G. Donders

ORBIS BOOKS

Maryknoll, New York 10545

The Catholic Foreign Mission Society of America (Maryknoll) recruits and trains people for overseas missionary service. Through Orbis Books, Maryknoll aims to foster the international dialogue that is essential to mission. The books published, however, reflect the opinions of their authors and are not meant to represent the official position of the society.

Library of Congress Cataloging-in-Publication Data

Donders, Joseph G.
    Christ, the divine network.

    Includes index.
    1. Bible.   N.T.   Gospels—Liturgical lessons,
English.   2. Bible.   N.T.   Gospels—Meditations.
I. Title.
BS2565.D65   1986   242′.5   86–718
ISBN 0–88344–254–X (pbk.)

This book is gratefully dedicated to
The Mothers' Union
of Saint Paul's Catholic University Chapel
Nairobi, Kenya
L. Byrne, E.W. Chege, M. Fernandez, A. Gethi, A.W. Kahara,
M.W. Kamau, S.W. Kariuki, V.N. Kariuki, S. Moloney,
B. Mutere, Ph. Muraga, N. Ngala, E.W. Nderitu, H. Odera,
and the whole of the
Saint Paul's Catholic Community.

CONTENTS

INTRODUCTION   1

1. THE TROUBLERS OF ISRAEL   5
(MATTHEW 24: 37-44; FIRST SUNDAY OF ADVENT)
2. PREGNANT WITH HOPE   9
(MATTHEW 3: 1-12; SECOND SUNDAY OF ADVENT)
3. DEPENDING DEPENDENCY   14
(MATTHEW 11: 2-11; THIRD SUNDAY OF ADVENT)
4. GOD-WITH-US   20
(MATTHEW 1: 18-24; FOURTH SUNDAY OF ADVENT)
5. HIS BIRTH IN US   26
(LUKE 2: 15-20; CHRISTMAS)
6. MARY MOTHER OF GOD   29
(LUKE 2: 16-21; FIRST SUNDAY AFTER CHRISTMAS)
7. EPIPHANY   34
(MATTHEW 2: 1-12; SECOND SUNDAY AFTER CHRISTMAS)
8. JOHN'S HOPE AND FRUSTRATION   37
(JOHN 1: 29-34; SECOND SUNDAY OF THE YEAR)
9. SINGING HIS SONG   42
(MATTHEW 4: 12-23; THIRD SUNDAY OF THE YEAR)
10. TELLING STORIES   45
(MATTHEW 5: 1-11; FOURTH SUNDAY OF THE YEAR)
11. YOU ARE THE SALT   50
(MATTHEW 5: 13-16; FIFTH SUNDAY OF THE YEAR)
12. NOT A THING   54
(MATTHEW 5: 17-37; SIXTH SUNDAY OF THE YEAR)
13. NEW VISION   58
(MATTHEW 5: 38-48; SEVENTH SUNDAY OF THE YEAR)
14. LIKE A LILY IN THE FIELD   61
(MATTHEW: 6: 24-34; EIGHTH SUNDAY OF THE YEAR)
15. KINGDOM WITHIN   65
(MATTHEW 7: 21-27; NINTH SUNDAY OF THE YEAR)
16. NOT ON BREAD ALONE   68
(MATTHEW 4: 1-11; FIRST SUNDAY OF LENT)

17. HOPE KEEPING US ALIVE   72
(MATTHEW 17: 1–9; SECOND SUNDAY OF LENT)

18. THE WAY TO GO   76
(JOHN 4: 5–42; THIRD SUNDAY OF LENT)

19. AREN'T WE BLIND?   80
(JOHN 9: 1–14; FOURTH SUNDAY OF LENT)

20. SAVED FROM DEATH   85
(JOHN 11: 1–45; FIFTH SUNDAY OF LENT)

21. BECAUSE OF THEIR FEAR FOR HIM   89
(MATTHEW 26: 14–27: 66; PALM/PASSION SUNDAY)

22. UP WILL PREVAIL   92
(JOHN 20: 1–9; EASTER SUNDAY)

23. UNDOING THE PAST   96
(JOHN 20: 19–31; SECOND SUNDAY OF EASTER)

24. BREAD BROKEN   100
(LUKE 24: 13–35; THIRD SUNDAY OF EASTER)

25. THE PRICE OF LOVE   104
(JOHN 10: 1–10; FOURTH SUNDAY OF EASTER)

26. RESURRECTION AND SOUP   107
(JOHN 14: 1–12; FIFTH SUNDAY OF EASTER)

27. WE WILL HAVE DONE IT   111
(JOHN 14: 15–21; SIXTH SUNDAY OF EASTER)

28. AND MARY THE MOTHER OF JESUS   115
(JOHN 17: 1–11; SEVENTH SUNDAY OF EASTER)

29. THE SHIFT IN THEM   120
(JOHN 20: 19–23; PENTECOST SUNDAY)

30. EMPOWERMENT   125
(JOHN 3: 16–18; TRINITY SUNDAY)

31. BODY OF CHRIST   130
(JOHN 6: 51–58; TWELFTH SUNDAY OF THE YEAR)

32. PETER AND PAUL   133
(MATTHEW 16: 13–19; THIRTEENTH SUNDAY OF THE YEAR)

33. REVEALED TO THE MEREST CHILDREN   137
(MATTHEW 11: 25–30; FOURTEENTH SUNDAY OF THE YEAR)

34. LOST ALONGSIDE THE ROAD   141
(MATTHEW 13: 1–23; FIFTEENTH SUNDAY OF THE YEAR)

35. LETTING GROW   145
(MATTHEW 13: 24–43; SIXTEENTH SUNDAY OF THE YEAR)

36. THE TREASURE IN YOU   149
(MATTHEW 13: 44–52; SEVENTEENTH SUNDAY OF THE YEAR)

37. WHAT WOULD JESUS HAVE DONE?   153
(MATTHEW 14: 13–21; EIGHTEENTH SUNDAY OF THE YEAR)

38. PRAYING AND LISTENING   157
(MATTHEW 14: 22–33; NINETEENTH SUNDAY OF THE YEAR)

39. NO STRANGER   161
(MATTHEW 15: 21-28; TWENTIETH SUNDAY OF THE YEAR)

40. DIVINITY IN ALL OF US   166
(MATTHEW 16: 13-20; TWENTY-FIRST SUNDAY OF THE YEAR)

41. TO SPREAD OUR ARMS   170
(MATTHEW 16: 21-27; TWENTY-SECOND SUNDAY OF THE YEAR)

42. RESPONSIBLE FOR EACH OTHER   174
(MATTHEW 18: 15-20; TWENTY-THIRD SUNDAY OF THE YEAR)

43. BREAD AND ROSES   179
(MATTHEW 18: 21-35; TWENTY-FOURTH SUNDAY OF THE YEAR)

44. HE SAID FRIEND   182
(MATTHEW 20: 1-16; TWENTY-FIFTH SUNDAY OF THE YEAR)

45. VISION AND LAW   185
(MATTHEW 21: 28-32; TWENTY-SIXTH SUNDAY OF THE YEAR)

46. THE EARTH IS OURS   188
(MATTHEW 21: 33-43; TWENTY-SEVENTH SUNDAY OF THE YEAR)

47. INVITED TOGETHER   191
(MATTHEW 22: 1-14; TWENTY-EIGHTH SUNDAY OF THE YEAR)

48. TRANSCENDING THEM   194
(MATTHEW 22: 15-21; TWENTY-NINTH SUNDAY OF THE YEAR)

49. OUR NEIGHBOR NOWADAYS   198
(MATTHEW 22: 34-40; THIRTIETH SUNDAY OF THE YEAR)

50. WHERE ARE YOU FROM?   202
(MATTHEW 23: 3-12; THIRTY-FIRST SUNDAY OF THE YEAR)

51. THAT MIDNIGHT CRY   206
(MATTHEW 22: 34-40; THIRTY-SECOND SUNDAY OF THE YEAR)

52. MINISTERING MONEY   210
(MATTHEW 25: 14-30; THIRTY-THIRD SUNDAY OF THE YEAR)

53. THE INHERITORS OF THE KINGDOM   214
(MATTHEW 25: 31-46; THIRTY-FOURTH SUNDAY OF THE YEAR)

INDEX OF SCRIPTURAL TEXTS   218

INTRODUCTION

Deep down in us,
in each one of us,
there is something
that makes it possible for us
to reach out of,
or into,
ourselves.
     From within that still point,
     we are able
     to touch
               —is it horizontally,
               is it vertically,
               is it diagonally,
               is it circularly,
               is it downward,
               is it upward,
               is it forward,
               is it backward,
               I don't know—
a reality
that the wise and the foolish
always
have been calling
God.
When we touch it,
we do not only touch,

or contact,
our deepest self
itself,
but also that Deepest Self
God-self.
    And reaching God,
    touching God-self,
    we touch at the same time
    all the others,
        in the present,
        in the past
        and in the future,
    who are like us,
    communicating,
    and participating
    in godliness,
    too.
This sacredness
was so wonderfully and exceptionally
present in Jesus of Nazareth
that it made his being
and his person
God's full manifestation
among us,
his fellow human beings.
    No wonder
    that he was called Christ,
    Chrestos,
    the anointed one,
    the one steeped in God,
    the one anointed by God,
    the one transparent with God,
    God with us,
    Emmanuel.
If he was called Christ
because of that realm
in him,
we should be called Christ,
or Christlike, too,

because what made him
what he was
is making us, too,
what we are,
in the deepest part of our being.
When Jesus reached out,
when Jesus contacted God,
in his unique way,
he contacted
at the same time
all those
in whom godliness
dwells.
Touching God,
he touched all of us.
The light that started to glow in him
made all of us shine
and see.
It is in that mysterious
—yet obvious—
way
that we all
are taken up in
a network,
the Jesus network,
or more precisely:
the Christ network,
connecting all of us.
That is why these reflections,
which were shared
with all kinds of people,
students and teachers,
old and young,
rich and poor,
hungry and satisfied,
in Baltimore and Dar es Salaam,
in Lusaka and Dublin,
in Paris and Nairobi,
in Lilongwe and Washington D.C.,

can be shared
with all of you,
with all of us,
in Jesus,
with whom we form
the Christ,
the new human being.

THE TROUBLERS OF ISRAEL

Matthew 24:37–44

You can prepare for Christmas
in very many different ways.
You can celebrate Christmas
as something that happened
in the past.
    It was in the past
    that Joseph and Mary traveled to Bethlehem,
    that they could not find a place in the inn.
    It was in the past
    that they finally found a shed,
    that Mary gave birth to her child.
    It was in the past
    that angels started to sing,
    that shepherds came to find the baby and his mother.
    It was in the past
    that some wise men came from the East,
    that Herod got upset about the newness announced.
    It was in the past
    that Jesus was circumcised in the temple,
    that Anne and Simeon came to greet him.

5

It was in the past
that the whole family finally had to flee
to the safety, the security, and the hospitality
of Africa.
You eat and drink
in a bar, a cafeteria, a restaurant,
or even at home,
as much as you can,
and even a bit more,
to commemorate that string of events
that took place so long ago,
once and for all,
in the past.
You can celebrate Christmas
as something that happens
in the present,
meditating upon the graces
given to you:
heaven opens again,
new life is given,
a saviour is born,
hope regained,
alleluia,
joy to the world!
Others celebrate it
by not celebrating it at all,
in protest,
or despair.
They say that Christmas did not help;
they say that Christmas does not help.
It has no meaning;
it had no meaning.
Nothing in the world ever changed,
no new life,
no salvation,
nothing at all.
They are
—apparently—
the ones without any hope,

without any expectation,
without anything.
Yet, they are the ones
who, maybe, do understand best
what Christmas is about.
They are the ones
looking for an alternative,
looking for a new beginning.
They seem to be the ones
most in line
with the expectations
expressed in the three readings of today:
the alternative offered
by Isaiah,
the alternative offered
by Paul,
the alternative offered
by Jesus himself.
Isaiah says:
"Come, let us go
to the mountain of the Lord,
let us walk in his paths,
let us come together,
let us hammer our swords into plowshares,
let us finish war."
Paul writes:
"The time has come,
the night is almost over,
it will be daylight soon.
Let us be awake
so that the light is not going to find us asleep."
Jesus says:
"Be prepared,
great things are going to happen,
get ready,
get ready!"
Those three appeals
do not ask us
to sit down, and eat, and drink,

celebrating only the past,
or merely the present.
We are urged to celebrate Christmas
in a way
that is directed to the future, too:
toward a change in our lives,
toward a change in the world,
walking to the mountain of the Lord,
growing in goodness, community, and peace
ever more.
When celebrating Christmas like that,
we will be joined
by all men and women of good will,
forming a pilgrim people
who are on the move.
We should not be settled
in the past of this world,
but not in its present either;
we should be:
"the troublers of Israel,"
a community of dissenters
in view of what Jesus came for,
in view of what the angels sang at his birth:
"Peace,
real peace,
his peace,
to all of humanity,
to all of the universe!"

2.

PREGNANT WITH HOPE

Matthew 3:1-12

John the Baptist was busy
in the river Jordan.
>They had come to him
>from all over the country.
>Some had come
>because it was "in" to go;
>but the majority had come
>in all sincerity.
>They came
>because they did not feel satisfied
>with their own lives;
>they came
>because they did not feel happy
>about the world in which
>they were living their lives.
They felt that something
should be done about them.
They felt that something
could be done about them.
>They were the ones
>who had not given up.

They were like the ones
Paul wrote about
in the reading of today:
the saints who had not given up,
people pregnant with hope
and full of endless joy.
John received them
without any formality.
He hardly greeted them.
It was only his message
that counted.
That is why he dressed
the way he was dressed:
in a skin he had found in the desert;
that is why he was eating
the way he was eating:
a handful of insects and some wild honey;
that is why he smelled
the way he smelled:
as the desert with those insects and that honey;
that is why he talked
the way he talked,
very abruptly:
    "Repent,
    the Kingdom is near!"
He baptized them,
one after another,
an endless row,
day after day,
strengthening the hope
of those
who had never given up.
    You can give up hope
    in different ways.
    You can give up on the road
    before you reach your aim
    because you are discouraged and frustrated.
    You can give up, too,

because you think
you are at the end of the road,
having reached your aim,
though you did not really:
like a student who leaves the university
after graduation day,
thinking he never has to open a book
again,
thinking that she has accomplished
all there is
to formation and education.
Those who had no hope anymore,
those who had given up
did not come to John.
They had told themselves
and each other:
"This world will always be the same."
They had nothing to look for
at that river Jordan.
But those others, too,
who had given up in that second way,
who thought themselves accomplished
in sanctity and holiness,
and who thought the world in which they lived
was as well organized as possible,
because they profited greatly
from things as they were,
did not come either.
They would hate any upheaval.
They were only interested
in the maintenance of the "status quo."
They lived too well;
they were not looking forward
to any change at all.
They came only at the moment
when John became a danger to them;
they came only at the moment
that John proved to be too successful.

They came
when hope began to grow
too much.
    So one day,
    John looked up
    and saw them standing there,
    Pharisees and Sadducees,
    on the brow of a hill,
    looking down on his work,
    and he shouted to them:
        "Brood of vipers,
        generation of snakes,
        who warned you to flee
        from the dangers to come?"
And he added,
indicating that he knew
what they were thinking:
"Don't say
nothing can happen to us,
we are saved and safe,
we are sons of Abraham.
It is not going to help you.
This world,
your world,
did come to an end.
It is going to change,
the Kingdom of God is going to come,
God's new invasion did start!"
    The Pharisees and Sadducees
    and all the others in power
    did not want that change.
    They were going to defend
    their position,
    even at the cost
    of the blood of Christ.
    That is what they implied
    at the moment they met John:
    they would fight
    to defend the existing stability,

the security, the law and order
protecting them.
Today
we are invited
to ask ourselves
to which group we belong:
   to the group
   of those who gave up
   and did not come,
   to the group
   of those who hardened their hearts
   and did not want to change,
   or to the group
   of those who did come
   because they were pregnant with hope
   and full of endless joy.
To which group do you belong?
Are you pregnant with hope?
Are you really pregnant with the hope
Mary was pregnant with
in the days we now celebrate:
ADVENT,
the coming of the Lord,
and the coming of the Kingdom of God?
   Are you pregnant
   like that?

3.

DEPENDING DEPENDENCY

Matthew 11:2–11

He was a student,
intelligent, powerful, and beautiful.
He told me some days ago
during a tutorial:
    "I don't like that Jesus;
    I don't like him to be the answer;
    I don't like him to have saved us;
    I don't like him to have redeemed us.
    If all they say about him is true,
    he did not leave anything to be done by us.
    He unnerved us;
    he emasculated us."
It is true that help is something
very ambiguous.
There is a difficulty
in all assistance and help.
As soon as someone is helped
there is the risk of dependency,
of total dependency,
and all efforts can stop.

Somewhere here in Kenya
there are six poles standing
in a field
just like that.
A local community
decided to build
a communal henhouse
in view of the proteins
they needed for their children.
It was not an easy job.
Materials were scarce,
but they started.
The first poles were in the ground,
connections were made.
All went as well as possible
until a group of overseas visitors
passed in a bus.
The bus stopped;
the tourists came out;
they saw the effort;
they admired it.
Some of them said
that they were even touched,
and they promised to send
some help
as soon as they arrived home.
They asked for the address of the community
and set off again.

    That very same day
    the building of the henhouse
    was stopped.
    People started to wait
    for the help
    that was going to come,
    and that never came.
Years ago
a professor here at the University
studied these dynamics
in view of the formulation
of a new national five-year plan.

According to his data
crippling of local efforts begins
at the moment
that even a fraction
of what one needs
comes from outside.
 If you as parents
 do not stop helping and assisting
 your children at a certain point,
 they may never do
 anything on their own.
 They may remain children;
 they may never grow up.
That must have been the reason
that their creator
left Adam and Eve alone
after having created them.
 God only came to visit them
 now and then
 at about five o'clock in the evening,
 when the wind from the south
 was cooling down.
 In those stories
 God respected them
 in their decisions,
 leaving it all to them.
Now God
had returned in Jesus Christ.
Was God going to take over?
Would Jesus change all and everything
with divine power
in one enormous move?
 That must have been
 what John was thinking
 in the solitude of his cell,
 in between four walls,
 chained to one of them,
 with some water and some bread,
 food he had not been accustomed to
 in the desert,

grasshoppers not being
on the prison's menu.
He must have been waiting
for the great takeover,
the big bang.
He didn't hear anything.
All seemed to be quiet.
Nothing seemed to happen.
    He sent his disciples
    to ask Jesus
    what he was doing,
    what he intended to do,
    when things would start to happen,
    whether he was the real one.
They came to Jesus.
They asked him John's questions,
and he answered,
not referring to his own work and activity,
but to the reaction and the activity
of the others:
    "Tell John
    that those who were blind see;
    that those who were lame walk;
    that those who had leprosy are healed;
    that those who were deaf hear;
    and that even those who seemed dead
    are seen walking in the streets again."
Life that seemed to have come to an end
had started to move.
People who seemed to have died
gave signs of life.
    It is, maybe, a bit too early
    to refer to the Christmas story.
    But in that story
    there are many incidents
    that illustrate God's policy.
Take all the stories about angels.
Those angels come to announce,
they come to warn,
but that is all they do;

that is all the support they offer,
they left the rest
to others.

>It is Mary
>who is bearing the child.
>It is Joseph
>who has to marry her.
>The shepherds have to walk
>on their own feet
>to the child.
>No transportation is provided.

The angel who comes to tell Joseph
that he has to pack up
and flee immediately with mother and child
leaves Joseph alone
to do the packing,
to organize the flight,
to saddle the donkey,
and to get the money
that was needed.
No further help
was given.

>Of course, that help was given,
>but it was given
>from within.
>It was given with respect
>for the persons involved.

Though depending on God,
they remained independent,
equipped from within
with all that was needed
to do
what was asked of them.
That independence
is the real glory
of God
in us.

>To John
>it seemed too slow;

he wanted to hasten things;
he wanted to see immediate results;
he wanted direct effects.
Jesus said:
"No,
the seed has been sown,
the fruits will follow.
Wait,
you have to be patient,
never lose heart.
The Lord is coming
soon."

4.

GOD-WITH-US

Matthew 1:18–24

Joseph
was in very bad shape.
He was depressed and upset,
in a panic and very sad.
>   His parents, and the parents of Mary
>   had been starting the wedding preparations
>   a year before,
>   as was proper, Jewish custom.
The contract had been signed.
They would have started living together
exactly a year after the signing.
He had been building their house
since that day.
>   Now, suddenly
>   —before that year was over—
>   Mary had returned
>   from her long visit to her aunt Elizabeth.
>   She obviously was with child
>   and Joseph had never been
>   with her.

20

He could have gone to the priests;
he could have accused her of unfaithfulness,
of adultery,
which would have meant
that Mary would have been stoned to death.
But he still loved her,
and that is why he decided
to divorce her
quietly.
Then, totally unexpectedly
that angel appeared to him,
an angel using a name
for the one Mary had conceived
in her womb:
"the one who saves the whole of the people."
Before Joseph wakes up
in the gospel story of today,
another name had been used for the child:
EMMANUEL,
God-with-us.
Those names
made Joseph change his mind;
those names
made him see the light;
those names
made him overcome his difficulties.
Hadn't God told Abraham:
"I will be your God?"
Hadn't God told Moses:
"I will be with you?"
Hadn't God foretold through Isaiah:
"A child will be born
from a virgin,
and his name will be:
GOD-WITH-US?"
Knowing those prophecies,
knowing his traditions,
Joseph did as he was told:

he took Mary to his home,
and finalized the marriage procedures.
 Those names
 had too much power
 to be taken
 lightly.
Words like these
have that power.
Let me tell you a story
to illustrate this.
 Somewhere on a new building site
 some children
 were playing football.
 Suddenly their ball,
 made of some old newspapers
 with a string of dry grass
 around them,
 disappeared behind a pile of rubble.
 One of the boys ran after it.
 A terrible scream was heard.
 When the others ran around the heap
 they saw what had happened:
 he had fallen into a very deep old dry pit.
 The sand around the pit was very loose.
 Every time they tried
 to get to the opening of the pit
 a lot of sand fell
 deep down below
 on the child below
 who was screaming like mad
 in total panic:
 "Help! Help!
 Father, mother,
 help! Help!"
Some grownups,
hearing the noise,
came running up,
but they did not know
what to do either.

Every time they approached the pit
sand fell down
and the child started to scream.
One of them ran to a telephone
in a nearby shop.
He called the fire department.
They arrived within a few minutes.
They put a long ladder
over the ground
towards the opening of the pit;
they threw a heavy string,
a kind of cable,
down the pit
and told the child
to tie it around himself.
The child
still in a panic
did not listen.
He just screamed and screamed.
Nobody dared to go down in the pit either;
the opening was too narrow
and the walls of the pit might collapse
on top of the child.

    Then another man came running
    to the scene.
    He crept over the ladder
    very slowly, and very carefully
    to the opening of the pit.
    He bent over the opening of the pit:
    "Joseph, be quiet.
    It is me, your father.
    I am with you.
    You are safe.
    Do what I tell you
    and you will get out."
When the child heard
his father's voice,
he calmed down;
the panic disappeared.

Here was someone
he trusted,
and when his father told him
to tie the cable around his chest,
under his armpits,
he listened.
That boy
saved himself
by listening to his father.
It was in that way
that Joseph,
the husband of Mary,
was saved through God's word.

    Friends,
    we are in that pit
    with darkness all around us.
    Many of us are in a panic
    in our personal lives,
    and all of us in our public lives
    because of scarcity, starvation, hunger,
    unemployment, frustration,
    missiles and rumors of war,
    many nice words,
    but no corresponding deeds:
    deep in a very dark
    pit.
Above the opening of that pit
there is now our Father,
God born among us
in Jesus Christ,
Jesus,
the-one-who-saves,
Emmanuel,
God-with-us.

    "Quiet, my daughter.
    Quiet, my son.
    I am with you,
    your father,
    your mother,
    your all.

Do what I say
and you will get out,
like Joseph did.
Amen."

5.

HIS BIRTH IN US

Luke 2:15–20

There is a very old legend.
Sometimes it is called
"the golden legend."
It tells how at the moment
of the birth of Jesus
time stopped.
>   The whole of nature
>   held its breath,
>   missed a beat,
>   stopped in its course.
The whole of creation
—from the minerals to the angels—
was aware
of what had happened.
>   It was made known to the earth
>   so the legend tells,
>   because an old temple in Greece
>   fell into dust that night.
>   It was made known to the water,
>   because a spring that flowed in Rome
>   changed into a fountain
>   of the finest oil.

26

It was made known to the plants,
for the vines in Spain
suddenly flowered, bore grapes,
and produced wine.
It was made known to the animals,
look at the oxen, the ass, the camels, and the sheep
around the manger.
It was made known to the birds,
for at the moment of his birth
all the cocks in the world
crowed in the middle of the night
at this new dawn.
It was made known to the angels,
because hosts of them
fluttered above the fields of Bethlehem,
making the news known
to the shepherds in those fields.
It was made known to the stars,
because even they started to move
in his direction.
Jesus was born,
but he was not the only one
to be born
that night.
    In all those minerals,
        those plants,
        those animals,
        those angels,
    but especially in all those human beings
    thronging around the manger,
    something else came to birth:
        in Mary,
        who sung it out first
        when she met her cousin Elizabeth;
        in Joseph,
        when he took Mary into his home;
        in the shepherds,
        when they started their search;
        in the wise men,
        when they began to follow the star;

in Simeon and Anne,
and in all those others,
in ourselves, too,
at the moment we joined
the movement
towards him.
They all had some hope
born into them,
born into us:
the Christ-like hope
that we will be able
to break through the night,
that we are going to change,
that we are not going to be left alone,
that God is with us,
Emmanuel.
A presence in us
will grow
more and more,
until all of us
will be Christlike,
like him,
JESUS,
the savior of the world.

6.

MARY MOTHER OF GOD

Luke 2:16–21

It is New Year's Day,
the beginning of a new year,
the beginning of a new period,
the beginning of a new era.
    You might say
    that this is exaggerated,
    that nothing will be new,
    that the newness of this first day
    is a figment of the imagination,
    that it all will remain the same.
It will not.
It will not be the same.
There will be variations,
variations on the old themes,
that may be true,
but variations, nevertheless:
    variations like those we hear in music,
    in African music,
    in Asian music,
    in Western music.

So often it is
one and the same theme,
repeated and repeated,
and repeated and repeated,
again and again,
all the time.
But each time
there is a small shift,
an insignificant new item,
a slight change in the melody,
a minimal difference in harmony,
the use of another instrument,
and that is why we can go on listening
to that same theme,
all the time,
endlessly,
up to the moment
that it all is changed
because of those little shifts,
and a new theme,
a new tune,
a new life,
sets in.
        It is such a newness
        we celebrate
        today.
        It is Mary
        we celebrate
        today:
        a village girl,
        the kind of village girl,
        you find all over the world.
        Variations,
        endless variations,
        an unbelievable number
        of variations,
        on that essentially
        same theme.

In this girl,
Mary,
something new started
when she must have been
about sixteen years old.
It happened in a scene
that since that time
has been painted and sculpted
over and over again.
        You know what happened to her:
        an angel appeared,
        announcing
        what would happen to this world,
        announcing
        that Jesus would be born into it,
        announcing
        that all would change,
        announcing
        a totally new development,
        announcing
        a new cosmic evolution,
        announcing
        a new creation,
        announcing
        an end to all pain,
                to all sorrow,
                to death itself.
And she,
from within herself,
said:
"Yes,
your will be done;
oh, yes,
your will be done!"
        —becoming pregnant
        with all newness to come.
And a song
started to sing in her,

a song whose words
she had collected
over the years
of her growing experience,
a song
in which she used
—again—
very old themes,
themes that had been used
for thousands and thousands of years.

> But because of what had happened to her,
> she sung
> those old themes
> in a new setting,
> in a new variation:

>> "My heart praises the Lord,
>> my soul is glad because of God my Savior,
>> for he has remembered me, his lowly servant.
>> From now on all people will call me blessed,
>> because of the great things
>> the mighty God has done to me.
>> His name is holy.
>> From one generation to another
>> he shows his mercy to those who honor him.
>> He has stretched out his mighty arm,
>> and scattered the proud with all their plans.
>> He has brought mighty kings from their thrones.
>> He has filled the hungry with good things,
>> and sent the rich away with empty hands.
>> He has kept the promise he made to our ancestors,
>> and has come to the help of his servant Israel.
>> He has remembered to show mercy to Abraham
>> and to all his descendants for ever."

Mary,
Miryam of Nazareth!
We put her on a throne;
we dressed her in gold and diamonds;
we invoke her;
we use her intercession with Jesus;

we gave her thousands and thousands of titles
in her litanies;
we built churches, cathedrals, and basilicas
in her honor.

> All this is explicable.
> It is, maybe, even justifiable.
> But the danger
> that she remains
> on that throne,
> in that dress,
> in that function,
> with those titles,
> in those churches,
> with her song,
> and her son,
> outside of you,
> is very great.

We should not
only invoke her,
and greet her;
we should not
only give her
all kinds of titles.

> We should sing
> her song
> from within us,
> as she did,
> from within herself.
> Amen.

7.

EPIPHANY

Matthew 2:1–12

There is a story about a concentration camp.
Two of the prisoners were looking out of the windows.
They looked from windows
in different blocks,
but they both looked
into the same dark night.
>It was very dark that night.
>You couldn't even see
>the fence and the trees
>around the camp.
>You couldn't even see
>the watchtowers
>with the soldiers and their machine guns
>on top.
One prisoner, looking into that endless darkness,
said to himself:
"I only see the darkness.
I only see mud.
I only see nothing."
>The other one, looking into that same darkness,
>said to himself:

34

"Look over there.
Look at those little lights.
Look at the stars."
And he pointed
at the vaguest of lights
that peeped through the darkness
of that night.
One was without hope;
the other one
had not lost his hope
at all.

When I told this story
during a service
at Kamithi Security Prison
in Nairobi,
I asked the prisoners:
"And what do you see
in the darkness of *your* night?"
Almost all of them,
the great majority of them,
shouted in unison:
"Stars, stars,
we see stars!"
Not all of them.
Each one of us
is like one of those two prisoners.
Each one of us is,
in a sense,
a prisoner in this world.

You meet people who,
when speaking
about their own affairs,
about our national affairs,
about our international affairs,
and even about our church affairs,
see only darkness,
disaster,
mud,
and despair.

You meet people who,
when speaking
about those same affairs,
see some light,
the light of so many stars,
the light of so many hopes.
Sometimes
those who see the light
are very few.
In the time of Christ's birth
there seem to have been
only three.
There might have been more,
maybe five or six,
but as only three gifts
are mentioned:
gold,
myrrh,
and incense,
we guess
that they were only three.
We even gave them three names:
Caspar,
Melchior,
and Balthasar.
In the dark of their night,
they saw the star,
the new hope.
That star brought out something in them,
something
that made them travel
all the way
from where they were
to Jesus.
It was their hope
that made their trip
possible.
Was it your hope
that brought you here?

8.

JOHN'S HOPE AND FRUSTRATION

John 1:29–34

John knew
that he was doing something
he could not do.
He was baptizing,
but he told them:
"This is not the real thing.
This is not really going to help you."
  He was like a man
  with a leaking roof.
  He had asked a roofer
  to come and have a look at it.
  The roofer said:
  "I can patch it;
  I can repair it;
  the worst will be over
  for some days,
  maybe,
  but you really need
  a completely new roof."

He was like that car owner
whose car did not work very well
anymore.
His mechanic told him:
"I can do something about it,
provisionally,
for the time being,
but what you really need
is a new motorblock.
That is what it needs."

    He was like that man
    in front of a doctor
    who listened to his heart
    and said:
    "I can give you some medicine.
    It will relieve you a bit,
    but what you really need,
    is a new heart,
    a completely new heart."

John knew, too,
that his impulse to baptize
did not come from him,
but from on high,
and that it would not be in vain
in the end,
that it would not be fruitless
all the time.

    One day
    humanity's shelters
    would be renewed;
    one day
    all human dynamism
    would be changed;
    one day
    the new heart would be given.

So he baptized
hundreds,
thousands,
tens of thousands,

in vain,
and not in vain,
without hope,
and yet full of hope.
And he must have been amazed
to see
how many
were hoping like he did,
for that new heart,
for that new drive,
for that new world.

John said:
"I came to baptize,
to reveal that breakthrough;
I came to baptize
that new human existence;
I came to baptize
because I live under the promise
that one day
I would see the Spirit
in one."
And that is what he saw
when Jesus was standing
in front of him.

Some years ago
we had a visitor
here in the chapel.
He was a Franciscan
from the United States.
His friends had organized
a meeting here in the chapel,
a charismatic meeting
at which he preached.
That preacher
was announced
all over town
on posters
and under his name
was printed:

"The John the Baptist
of the Twentieth Century."
        That was understandable.
        It was a nice comparison,
        and yet
        it was a mistake;
        it was an anachronism;
        it was a mixing up
        of times.
Among you,
among us,
nobody should preach anymore
as John the Baptist,
because in you,
because in us,
that very same Spirit of Jesus
is present.
It is very often
unknown,
unnoticed,
forgotten,
and even frustrated,
but it is there.
        There is a German author,
        the Nobel prize winner for literature in 1946,
        Hermann Hesse,
        who was very interested in peace,
        and who wrote
        that he did not believe
        that peace would be brought about
        by conferences,
        preaching,
        organizations,
        or propaganda.
        He wrote:
        "Like all human progress,
        the love of peace
        must come from knowledge:

the knowledge of the living substance in us,
in each one of us,
in you and in me,
the secret godliness
that each of us
bears within him or her."
And he added
that it was that knowledge
that appeared in our fellow human being
Jesus
in a glorious way.
That godliness
is in all of us.
It is the reason
that we belong together,
that even our enemies
are our sisters and brothers.
That is the world
John
was baptizing for;
that is the world
the others
wanted to be baptized for.

9.

SINGING HIS SONG

Matthew 4:12–23

Jesus was in Judea
when John the Baptist was arrested.
He was in the same region
in which John was detained.
> He decided to get out of Judea
> and to go to Galilee.
> He went to Capharnaum
> and settled there.
Why did he choose Galilee?
We don't know,
but there are some hints
in the gospel of today
that might help us
to understand his choice.
> Galilee was a very open province.
> It was the least Jewish region
> of the Jewish regions.
> That is why it was called
> Galilee of the pagans,
> or Galilee of the Nations.

He went to Galilee,
but not to his old Galilean home town
of Nazareth.
he went to Capharnaum,
not a very large town,
but not a very small town either.
It was a harbor
with a lot of traffic,
a very open town
with a mixed population.
Some commentaries state
that it was as cosmopolitan a town
as a city of that size,
in that time,
could be.
>Capharnaum,
>in those days,
>was the Jewish window
>to the world.

He picked
the least Jewish town
in the least Jewish region
of Palestine.
>It is there
>that he started to preach.
>It is there
>that he started to sing his song:
>>*"Repent,*
>>*the Kingdom of God*
>>*is at hand!*
>>*Reform,*
>>*we will overcome!"*

Preaching that news,
singing that song,
he was surrounded by people
from all over the world;
he was surrounded
by Jews, Romans, and Greeks,
by Africans and Asians.

And suddenly a miracle occurred,
the message he gave,
the song he sung,
lifted them up from within;
they recognized their own desires;
they heard their own voices;
and his song
was no longer confined
to him.
It became the song
of them all.
It was no longer clear
what kind of song it was,
his or theirs,
African or Jewish,
Asian or Roman,
though it remained the song
Isaiah had already sung before:
"Anguish will take wings,
darkness will be dispelled,
gloom will fade,
distress will disappear,
a light will shine,
joy will reign,
the yoke will be taken away,
the rod will be smashed,
freedom for all,
we will overcome!"
They sung that song;
they sung it together
as he taught them to do,
as we are taught,
too.

10

TELLING STORIES

Matthew 5:1–11

Three visitors came to me
some days ago.
They came from very far;
they came from France.
I forgot their names;
I saw them only once.
    They came to ask me
    what I thought of their plan.
    I asked them
    what their plan was.
    They said that they came
    in view of the Fourth World.
    I asked them:
    "What is the Fourth World?"
    They answered:
    "They are the ones
    who are forgotten
    in the Third World."
I asked them
what they intended to do
with those poorest of the poor.

They said:
"We would like to live with them
and tell them stories."
I said:
"Tell them stories?"
"Yes,"
they answered,
"to show them
who they are."
"Isn't that,"
they added,
"what the Bible stories
and what the stories of Jesus do
all the time?
If people knew
who they are,
they would be able to do
wonderful things.
They would be able
to help themselves
out of their frustrations and difficulties."
> When I told them
> that I still did not understand,
> they told me
> how Moses talked
> one of the most frustrated human groups,
> the Jewish slaves in Egypt,
> out of their misery.
> At the moment they believed
> what Moses told them about themselves
> —in the name of Jahweh—
> they were able to save themselves.
They told me
how Jesus spoke
in such a way
that those who listened
picked up hope
and said to themselves
and to each other:

"We are going to make it.
Oh yes, we will!"
And they gave as an example
the gospel of today.
>   Jesus was surrounded
>   by people
>   who had come from very far
>   to see him
>   and to hear him.
He got lost in the crowd
that surrounded him,
that touched him,
that was so full of hope
that he was going to change
their lives.
>   He climbed the hill
>   so that he was a bit above them
>   and so that all could see him,
>   and he sat down.
>   The twelve sat down around him,
>   careful not to block his view,
>   and not the crowd's view either.
He looked at the crowd,
so eager,
so simple,
so hopeful.
He looked in their faces,
the faces of old men and women,
marked by the intensity of their lives;
the faces of mothers and fathers,
all the time looking anxiously around
not to lose their children;
he looked at the younger ones
who looked at him,
but who at the same time
could not stop looking at each other,
so full of hope
in the new life
bubbling in them.

He looked at them,
and he was reminded of so much
he had experienced
growing up in Nazareth
with people like these;
he was reminded of his mother Mary,
of Joseph,
and he said,
thinking of all of them:

>"How happy are the poor in spirit,
>theirs is the kingdom of heaven.
>Happy are the gentle,
>they shall have the earth for their heritage.
>Happy are those who mourn,
>they shall be comforted.
>Happy are those who hunger and thirst for what is right,
>they shall be satisfied.
>Happy are the merciful,
>they shall have mercy shown them.
>Happy are the poor in heart,
>they shall see God.
>Happy are the peacemakers,
>they shall be called sons and daughters of God.
>Happy are those who are persecuted in the cause of right,
>theirs is the kingdom of heaven."

They listened;
at first they did not understand,
but then they understood.
Slowly it dawned upon them:
he was speaking of them,
he was speaking about them at their best,
he was speaking about them at their fullest,
he was speaking about all the good
hidden in them.

>They must have gone home that day
>knowing better
>who they were,
>what they were able to do; .

they went that day
full of hope,
and with a tremendous joy.
But they must have been shocked, too,
knowing how rarely they lived up
to their human dignity.
They had heard God's word
on them,
and so did we,
on us.

11.

YOU ARE THE SALT

Matthew 5:13–16

It is sometimes in letters,
other times over the telephone,
or even at a party,
that people say that they left the church.
Very often they explain why,
    and although the reasons are always different,
    the main reason is very often the same,
    just as all human beings
    are in everything almost the same.
A letter I got some days ago
expressed that reason as follows:
    "Many preachers do nothing other than
    remind us
    that we are in fact sinners,
    and then they quote
    some verses from the Bible,
    reminding us
    of the sufferings
    ahead of us."
I don't know whether they are right;
I don't hear many sermons myself.

But considering the frequency of that remark,
there must be some truth in it.
But not biblical truth.
>That is really not the way
>that Jesus spoke about us.
>Jesus is more positive.
>Today he tells us:
>"You are the salt.
>You are the light.
>You are the city on the mountaintop!"
He does not say:
"You should be!"
He says:
"You are!"
And he explains what would happen to this world
if we forget.
>Read the first letter of John
>to his community,
>a community that most probably
>consisted of a few hundred
>scattered followers of Jesus.
>He writes:
>>"For the darkness is passing away,
>>and the real light is shining."
He was so convinced
of the internal power
awakened in those Christians
that he did not hesitate to write this,
though those Christians
were like a few small stars
in the darkness
of the world
in which they lived.
>You, too, know of that power.
>I am sure you have experienced it,
>or heard about its experience.
A girl came to me.
She was very upset.
She was scared stiff;

she said that she did not know
what to do.
I asked her
what had happened.
She told me how she was convinced
that something evil had struck her,
not only her,
but even her mother and her grandmother.
> She had gone
> to what she called
> a witchdoctor
> who had given her all kinds of powders,
> potions,
> and strange things.
> She got more and more afraid.
> She went more and more to that man.
> She broke out in tears
> and told me
> that she wanted to be liberated
> from all that,
> and she asked me
> if I could come to her house
> to take all those strange things away,
> and burn them.
> She said
> she would never dare to do that by herself.
I went to her house.
I asked her to put everything
in a paper bag.
She went through her house,
and from everywhere
she got those things together.
She said:
"I won't dare to throw them away."
We prayed together,
reminding ourselves in that prayer
how we have God's power in us.
After that prayer,
she took the paper bag
and put it outside of her house.

When she realized what she had done,
she broke out in tears.
 God's power in us.
 It is of that power
 that Isaiah speaks
 in the first reading of today;
 it is of that power
 that Paul writes
 in the second reading of today;
 it is of that power
 that Jesus speaks in the gospel.
  All three
  want to restore to us
  our proper dignity;
  all three want to show us
  our possibilities.
We should listen to them;
we should believe them;
and we should believe in ourselves.
Living accordingly.

12.

NOT A THING

Matthew 5:17–37

A small boy was kicking
a doll.
I could not see that it was a doll;
to me it seemed to be only a piece of dark wood.
A small girl was trying to get at
the doll.
She was shouting:
    "Don't kick her!
    It is my doll!
    It is Lucy,
    it is Lucy."
But the boy kept on kicking,
shouting:
    "It is not Lucy.
    It is only a thing,
    a thing . . . ,"
and he kicked,
and kicked.
    Do you remember
    a photo in the *Daily Nation*
    a few days ago?

54

It showed a man
on his face in the street,
surrounded by a mob.
Some policemen were guarding him.
Under the photo was a caption
that stated
that he was a thief
and the police had come just in time
to save him
from being beaten to death,
from being lynched in the street
by an angry mob.
But they had not come in time
to prevent the crowd
from cutting off one of his fingers.
The man was lying flat on the street
with an outstretched arm,
looking at his hand
in front of him.
In the gutter of the street
was something that looked
like the stump of a cigar:
his cut-off finger.
And wasn't there a story
some time ago
that not far from here
a girl returning from a hotel
was captured, stripped,
and tossed up
in a crowd
like an ugly despicable thing,
      a beautiful girl,
         with body and soul,
            with spirit and content divine,
tossed up just like that,
high up in the air,
like a ball
to be manhandled
by all.

It is about this type of event,
it is about those issues,
it is about these situations,
it is about those horrible possibilities,
that Jesus is speaking
today.
Jesus says,
Christ says:
"Don't make your brother into a fool.
Don't make your sister into a thing!"
One of the most horrible episodes
in Africa's struggle for independence
and self-determination
was the freedom fight in North Africa.
So many people were tortured, maimed, and killed,
that some doctors, psychologists, and psychiatrists
—Frantz Fanon was one of them—
started to wonder
how this inhuman behavior was possible.
They did some research
and they found out
that no one ever tortured a human being
just like that.
Before the police,
         the soldiers,
         or the public,
started to kick and to beat,
before they *could* start to beat,
something else had to happen
first.
They had to declare their victim
a non-human being.
         They would shout, "Pig,"
         and then they could beat.
         They would shout, "Dog,"
         and then they would be able to kick.
         They would shout, "Vermin," or "Insect"
         and then they would be able to kill,
         to crush under their feet.

Jesus in the gospel of today pleads:
"Don't do that;
don't call each other names!
Respect each other.
If you don't do that,
you are all going
to get hurt,
those who are kicked
and those who kick."
        That was the very observation
        of Frantz Fanon.
        Being a practicing psychiatrist,
        one day
        he received a man
        who was upset, depressed, and low,
        who could hardly sleep during the night,
        and who when sleeping had terrible nightmares
        because he had been treated
        as a non-human being,
        because he had been tortured
        as if he were a thing.
Another day, he received a man
who was upset, depressed, and low,
who could hardly sleep during the night,
and who when sleeping had terrible nightmares
because he had kicked others
as if they were things,
because he had acted
as a non-human being.
        It is our own sanity,
        it is our own dignity,
        it is our own health,
        it is our own existence
        that is at stake.
"Don't do it!
Don't make each other
into a thing.
Never!"

13.

NEW VISION

Matthew 5:38–48

It was
an eye for an eye,
a tooth for a tooth,
a hand for a hand,
a slap for a slap,
a kick for a kick
—a circle of violence,
turning around and around
without any end—
and he said:
>*"It should stop.*
>*Turn the other cheek."*

It is
a gun for a pistol,
a machine gun for a gun,
a bomb for a machine gun,
a missile for a bomb,
an atomic bomb for a missile,
a neutron bomb for an atomic one,
an antideterrent for a deterrent,
an anti-antideterrent . . . ,
an endless race,

a senseless race,
a murderous race,
no longer in a circle
but in a growing spiral of violence,
without any end,
and he said:
> *"Love each other,*
> *break out of that race,*
> *be friends,*
> *wish each other well."*

We did not listen,
but went further and further,
higher and higher,
even up into space,
watching and controlling,
checking and counterchecking,
spying and double-crossing
each other,
spending
almost all we had,
and have,
on possible destruction,
the final solution,
total extermination,
the holocaust.

> But while our scouts,
> spies sent from our divided world,
> were high up there
> in the solitude
> of freezing ice-blue sky,
> alone and on their own,
> they had a vision
> others had had
> long before.

They saw their earth
—that divided place
they came from,
so far and so small—
dressed in blue and white,
the virgin-mother of all,

of friends and foes,
of Americans and Russians,
of black and white,
and seeing her,
that goodly frame of all,
that little " ◯ "
they understood
that it simply does not make sense
to speak and think
in terms of divisions,
of borders,
of walls,
of barbed wire.
They saw the earth
as their common mother,
genetrix,
on whom
—as Jesus had seen before—
the heavenly father
pours his life-giving rain
over the good and the bad,
to make us grow
—in the light of the sun—
once and for all,
into the oneness
we were created in from all eternity,
escaping from all
that divides,
now
and for all time
to come.

14.

LIKE A LILY IN THE FIELD

Matthew 6:24–34

"Old King Solomon had a thousand wives,
and that is the reason why,
he never kissed them all,
when he said good-bye."
>   Did you ever hear
>   what King Solomon,
>   his seven hundred wives from royal stock,
>   and his three hundred concubines,
>   plus their combined staff
>   ate
>   in one day?
We know;
the Bible tells us.
It gives us
in the First Book of Kings
one page out of the household-book
of King Solomon's kitchen:
>   Thirty measures of fine flour,
>   sixty measures of meal,
>   ten fattened oxen,
>   twenty-three free-grazing oxen,

one hundred sheep,
plus deer, gazelles,
roebucks, and fattened fowl.
All this was eaten
from golden plates.
Solomon was the wisest human person
who ever lived.
He composed 3,000 proverbs,
and wrote 1,500 poems.
He could lecture on plants
from a cedar in Lebanon
to the simple hysop
growing from a wall.
He could talk on animals,
on birds,
on reptiles,
and on fish.
From all over the world
people came to witness
his astounding knowledge.
He was pious,
and built an unforgettable temple;
he was business-minded,
and monopolized the whole arms-trade
in his part of the world;
he was a warrior
who never lost a battle,
with his 1,400 war chariots,
and his 12,000 horses. . . .
And yet,
Jesus says
that Solomon in all his array
was nothing
in comparison
to a simple bird
flying high up in the sky,
to the splendor of a flower
out in the field,
or even to a blade of grass

Jesus does not set Solomon
as our example,
but that bird,
that flower,
that blade of grass.
Like those things
we should not worry
about what to eat,
about what to drink,
about how to dress,
like Solomon must have done;
we should be different.
      Jesus does not say
      that we should not eat,
      that we should not drink,
      that we should not dress;
      but he does say
      that our splendor
      should not come
      from all that.
"Unbelievers
are always running
after these things,
but you,
you should be seeking
the Kingdom of God,
the Kingdom of God
that
is
within":
      as it is
      in that bird;
      as it is
      in that flower;
      as it is
      in that blade of grass,
      shining forth
      from within.
Anything you are running after,

anything you chase,
runs ahead of you,
outside of you,
and it will never make
you
shine.

>   Our splendor comes
>   from what is chasing
>   us:
>   God
>   and his Kingdom
>   from within.

Be like a flower,
a lily in the field:
shining from within,
from within God
in you.

15.

KINGDOM WITHIN

Matthew 7:21-27

It was at a reception
somewhere in Nairobi.
He was standing
not too far from me.
Suddenly he raised his voice
and I felt
that he did this
to be heard by me,
and he said:
    "The missionary success in Africa
    is a disaster.
    It will be like all over the world:
        the church
        will pray with them,
        will sing with them,
        will forgive their sins,
        will chase their demons,
        will heal their wounds,
        keeping them poor,
        and low,
        and underdeveloped."

When he finished
he looked at me
just when I looked at him,
and now I was sure
what he said
had been meant for me.
When I looked away
I heard him add:
> "Think of the situation
> in South and Central America!
> Isn't that
> what they did?"
>> I think that he was right,
>> and that the church leadership often
>> was wrong with their
>> "Lord, Lord,"
>> their prophesying,
>> their excorcising,
>> their healing,
>> overlooking something
>> more fundamental
>> than all that:
>> the Kindom of God
>> in them.
Jesus, too, had said:
"Lord, Lord,"
he prophesied,
he exorcised,
he healed,
but again and again
he spoke
about a reality in *them*
that had to grow:
> a seed that had been sown,
> a pearl that was hidden,
> a net bringing life from the depth of the sea,
> a householder finding old and new in his stock.
He tried to convince
all of them

that his word and his life
had been planted in them,
had been planted in all of us,
and that God,
and his reign,
should grow
from within.
　　It is not from the words of others,
　　neither from their healings,
　　nor from their exorcisms,
　　that we should grow.
　　It is from within,
　　from his word and his life
　　in us
　　that we should grow
　　doing his will
　　from within.

16.

NOT ON BREAD ALONE

Matthew 4:1–11

He went into the desert
—so the story goes—
for forty days.
He went there
to make the switch,
to leave the life
he had been living
and the world
as it had been.
    He wanted to begin
    anew;
    he wanted to receive
    the Spirit,
    who descended into him.
By peeling off the old,
he hoped to reach
the human core,
the beginning of all.
    After forty days,
    helped by angels
    sent from God,

he was prepared,
ready to go,
ready to start
a new life,
a new world,
the Kingdom of God.
It was at that
very vulnerable moment
that another angel
came along,
not sent by God,
but authorized nevertheless:
the adversary,
the enemy,
the counterforce,
the devil,
Satan.
Seeing his hunger
and his willingness
to feed all,
that devil said:
"Why not take the easy solution?
Why not turn
stones
into bread?"
Indeed,
an easy way out.
He, himself, would be fed,
and all the others,
too.
But for the rest,
nothing would be done.
All the structures
that caused the hunger
in the world
in which he lived
—and in the world
in which we would live—
would not be taken away
in the least.

People would eat,
that is true;
but life would not change.
Injustice and sin,
laziness and greed,
would not be taken away;
oppression and exploitation
would continue to grow.
Nothing really
would have been done.
He looked at the devil;
he looked at the stones;
he felt the hunger in his stomach;
he felt the pain in the stomachs
of all those
who were, and are, and will be hungry,
and he decided:
"No, I am not going to do that."
He said:

> "Humanity does not live
> on bread alone,
> but on all that comes from the mouth
> of God!"

He must have thought
of what he would pray for
later in his life:

> "Our Father,
> who art in heaven,
> your Kingdom come,
> your will be done on earth,
> as it is in heaven.
> Give us today
> our daily bread."

It is only in that Kingdom
that bread is assured
for all.

> Daily bread
> is bread for every day.
> Daily bread means
> the eradication of hunger.

Daily bread means
the removal of the oppression and exploitation
that caused the hunger in his days,
and that causes the hunger in our days.
Daily bread means
moving and changing heaven and earth,
including the unjust structures
in which we try to live together.
Daily bread,
his daily bread,
does not come
the easy way;
it comes
a difficult way.
That is what he knew,
launching out
in this world,
assembling us
around his cause.

17.

HOPE KEEPING US ALIVE

Matthew 17:1–9

Those who followed him
thought they knew
what they were in for.
They did not follow him
for nothing.
They were going to witness
the establishment
of the Kingdom of God here on earth.
Here on earth.
No more,
and no less.
    Every blind man who saw,
    every deaf woman who heard,
    every mute child who talked
    was for them
    another sign
    of things to come.
    It was as clear as that.
Of course,
they really did not know
what they were in for.

They had no idea;
they could not have had any idea
of the change-over
that would take place
around him.
How he
who healed the blind
would be blinded
by a crown of thorns;
how he
who healed the deaf
would be deafened
by the blows on his head;
how he
who healed the mute
would be silenced,
hanging on a cross,
paralyzed in all his movements
by nails
through his hands and his feet.
They had no idea
that their expectations
would be drowned
in the water and the blood
streaming from that cross.
Was that the reason
why
he brought them
to that mountaintop?
Was that the reason
why
he was transfigured
in front of them?
At the moment of that change
they did not need
any hope.
Hope does not count
when we believe we are sure of the answers,
when we believe we are certain of the solutions.

Hope was not needed
as long as he was with them,
energizing and preaching,
healing and exorcising,
manifesting his forceful
and dynamic, divine personality.
Hope
is needed
when night and darkness
fall,
when the way ahead
is totally obscured,
when no answer
seems possible,
when any solution
seems absurd.
It is in those moments
that hope,
and hope alone,
can help us
to carry on,
marching into the heart
of the struggle.
They would need hope
when seeing him hanging
in the darkness
of that frightful Friday night.
We, his followers, need hope
when seeing humanity itself
in agony,
crucified
by the oppression of two-thirds of the world
by one third,
by the spending of almost all human resources
on nuclear-death preparations,
by the exploitation of the poor,
causing hunger and starvation
all over the world.

Wasn't that the reason
that
he allowed them to see
what the final outcome
would be?
I think so.
Don't you think so,
too?
He did not reason,
reasoning would be lost
in the dark of those nights;
he did not make a promise,
promises would have remained idle words
facing the despair of the millions;
he *showed* what would happen
by making it happen
there and then,
and he said:
"Don't tell the others
before I come through death myself;
but then,
tell them!"
It was the hope
he left to us all.
It is with that hope
that we should struggle in this world,
and in ourselves.
We will not only overcome,
but one day
we,
you and I,
and all of us,
the whole of humankind,
we will be transfigured.
We will
shine
as he did,
and does.

18.

THE WAY TO GO

John 4:5–42

To know one's destination,
one's journey's end,
is all important.
We have to know where to go
to be able to arrive.
>   He revealed our goal
>   the day he started to shine
>   in front of them,
>   on top of that hill.
>   Remaining the same,
>   keeping his body
>   and the features
>   that had marked him
>   so far,
>   he was transformed
>   in glory,
>   divine.
Knowing one's destination,
one's journey's end,
is not sufficient.

We have to know the path
to be able to arrive.
    One day
    he arrived
    at the Samaritan town of Sechem.
    It was noon.
    They had walked all morning
    in the brilliant sun.
    He was tired,
    hungry, and thirsty.
    And as we all want
    when being hungry and thirsty,
    first he wanted
    something to drink.
    They arrived at a pit,
    an old Jacob's well.
    He sent his disciples off
    to buy something to eat
    and something to drink.
    He sat down at the well.
    Though he smelled the water,
    he had no way
    to reach it,
    until she came.
He should not have spoken to her.
It was against all custom.
Men did not address women in public.
A Jew never spoke to a Samaritan,
whether man or woman.
He should have left her alone.
The walls
separating him as a man
from her as a woman,
the circles
surrounding him as a man
and her as a woman,
should have remained
unbroken,
untouched.

That is how it was,
that is how it had been,
that is how it should be,
for ever and ever.
    She was not surprised
    that the Jewish tourist
    spoke to her
    as a *woman*.
        His disciples, afterwards,
        would be very surprised,
        and even scandalized by it.
    She was accustomed
    to being accosted by men
    in lonely and hidden places,
    otherwise she would never had had
    the relations she had
    with so many of them.
    That type of propriety
    was not her foremost concern.
But she was very surprised,
that this Jewish man
spoke to her
as a *Samaritan* woman.
How was this possible?
How could she,
a Samaritan,
give a drink
to this man,
a Jew?
    To stick to her religious laws,
    to those types of taboos,
    was to her more important
    than anything else,
    definitely more important
    than his thirst.
That day,
in the light of sun at noon,
Jesus struck
at the three walls

that even now
separate us most,
three barriers
that hinder us,
up to now,
from shining
in glory
together:
    the discrimination
    of women by men,
    the discrimination
    of race by race,
    the discrimination
    of religious institution by religious institution.
Jesus was thirsty,
asking for a drink,
breaking through the barriers
that cause humanity's thirst
even today.
    What he asked for
    was not given
    that day
    because his disciples came back,
    interrupting
    the conversation,
    the dialogue,
    the communion
    he had started,
    as we are still interrupting him
    in the fulfilment of his desire
    all the time.
His thirst
is still there,
though he showed us
what to do,
how to reach our goal,
and shine.

19.

AREN'T WE BLIND?

John 9:1–14

Speaking about blindness,
Jesus does not have much of a message
for most of us.
Aren't almost all of us
seeing?
> The Pharisees thought so, too.
> That is why they said:
> "You don't count us in
> with the blind,
> do you?"
And he said:
"If you were blind,
there would be no sin in that.
'But we see,' you say,
and your sin remains."
> We are not blind,
> but do we see,
> do we really see?
I think
that very many of us
have what is called
tunnel-vision:

a vision
that is restricted
to one line,
to one direction,
to certain things.
We don't see it all,
we only see part,
and often we miss
the most important part,
the part
that really counts.

     There were three people
     from up-country
     who came to town.
     They came from up-country,
     to the big town,
     Nairobi.
They came from a very small place,
in fact it was hardly a place at all.
If there had been a road
—there wasn't—
you could have easily passed their place
without ever noticing anything.

     But in that place
     there lived a tailor,
          a shoemaker,
          a clergyman,
          and a teenager.
     There lived more people,
     but the story is about
     those four.
They had decided
to go to town.
They had been saving for a long time,
and finally they had enough money
to make it.
They went.

     After some days
     they returned,
     all four of them.

And all four of them
were surrounded by friends
and relatives
who had never had
enough money
to be able
to go to town.
They wanted to hear
their stories.
They all had
the same story.
They all told
the same thing:
Nairobi is unbelievable,
Nairobi is wonderful,
Nairobi is simply fantastic.
    The tailor said:
    "Nairobi is wonderful.
    You should see the clothing
    the people wear
    in that town!
    Oh man,
    I wish I were a tailor
    in Nairobi!"
The shoemaker said:
    "Nairobi is great.
    You should see the shoes
    the people wear
    in that town!
    Oh boy,
    I wish I were a shoemaker
    in that town!"
The clergyman said:
    "My dear sisters and brothers,
    my friends in Jesus Christ,
    Nairobi is heavenly.
    You should see the crowds
    in the churches.
    Alleluia, alleluia.
    Praise the Lord!

        I wish I were a preacher
        in Nairobi!"
And the teenager,
surrounded by his friends and classmates,
said the same thing:
        "Nairobi, man,
        just the thing!
        You should have seen the discos
        and the girls!
        Wow! Wow!"
They all had been there;
they all had seen it.
And yet none had been there
and none had seen it.
They all had been suffering from
tunnel-vision.
        One had seen the clothing,
        and nothing else;
        one had seen the shoes,
        and nothing else;
        one had seen the churches,
        and nothing else;
        one had seen the young folks,
        and nothing else.
        Seeing,
        they had been blind.
Jesus seems to suggest
in the gospel of today
that we are blind,
too.
And aren't we?
Aren't we so occupied
        with our daily worries
        that we don't see
        what is happening around us?
        Aren't we so occupied
        with ourselves
        that we don't see
        how the grace of God
        is jumping,

or better,
trying to jump on us
all the time?
We don't see,
and God's graces are so many:
a beautiful day,
the face of your child,
the love you enjoyed,
the color of the field,
the friendliness you received,
the comfort you gave,
the right word you managed to find,
the food you ate. . . .
Let us not be blind,
let us not have tunnel-vision,
let us be open to God,
let us be his children,
seeing divinity and grace
in the world
in which we live.

20.

SAVED FROM DEATH

John 11:1–45

Everyone of us knows
about escaping from something,
only to be caught by it again.
> You have an old car;
> it stops on you
> so you bring it in for repairs.
> You go to get it.
> All goes very well,
> and yet you know
> that one day
> you will have to go to that garage
> again.
You have a toothache.
You go to the dentist
but you don't like to.
And you have to go back
several times.
You are looking forward to the last time.
Finally he puts all his drills and brushes away.
Your toothache is relieved;
your teeth are okay.

The dentist says:
"That is it.
I will send you the bill."
You leave his place
full of pep,
glad and happy,
feeling your teeth with your tongue.
The world seems to you
renewed and refreshed,
and yet you know
that one day
you will have to go back
again.

>It must have been
>something like that
>for Lazarus.
>He was brought back to life;
>he was awakened,
>not because he had asked for it,
>but because his sisters did.

Did he want to come back?
Nobody knows;
the gospel
does not say.

>One thing is sure:
>he had to die again.
>Jesus did not really save
>him from death.
>Just like that car mechanic
>did not really solve
>all your car problems;
>just like that dentist
>did not really get rid of
>all tooth decay.
>Lazarus would have to die again,
>and in fact
>he did.

But Jesus had shown
that death was not the disaster
people often thought it to be.

Jesus had shown them,
and us,
that when we die,
we don't disappear.
We don't fall
into nothingness.
We still will be there.
        Jesus had shown them,
        and us,
        that we never will die,
        because we are like Lazarus,
        his friend.
Some days ago,
an old man came to me.
He was very sad;
he said that his doctor had told him
that he was going to die
very soon.
        He told me:
        "I don't mind dying.
        I am very old.
        My time has come.
        I am not afraid.
        But I love my family
        and I love my friends.
        That is what
        I am going to miss."
The gospel of today
shows that this fear
is without ground.
Lazarus
came back
because his sisters
wanted him back,
because Jesus
his friend
called him back.
        All his relations
        and friendships
        he had taken with him.

Lazarus came back
because of them.
Jesus himself said
that what we call death
is only a sleep,
that we will never really die
because we remain
with him,
and he
with us.

21.

BECAUSE OF THEIR FEAR FOR HIM

Matthew 26:14–27:66

He had said
that he would be delivered
into the hands
of men.
He was.
    They all had shouted
    "Alleluia"
    as long as things went well,
    as long as they needed him,
    as long as he seemed a help to them,
    as long as he healed
    their ears and their eyes,
    their fits and their convulsions,
    their limbs and their bones.
They all stopped singing
"Praise the Lord"
as soon as he was caught
by those who envied him his influence
and who were scared
to lose their own power.

89

All those in authority
had the same fear:
the priests as well as the doctors,
the kings as well as the viceroys,
the military as well as the Pharisees.
It was their fear
that brought them together
against him.
It was their fear
that brought them together
against all those
who had been surrounding him,
singing alleluia,
waving their palms
and their flowers,
spreading out their dresses
and their carpets,
showing their children
and their pets.
Hadn't he
stimulated them,
continuously,
to be themselves?
Hadn't he tried,
incessantly,
to transform them
into real men and women,
independent and self-reliant?
Hadn't he
made them conscious,
fearlessly,
of their role in history?
It was in their fear
of that *conscientization*
that they became friends
in order to undo
him,
as they always have been doing,
and are still doing
today:

the colonial powers
and its collaborators,
the popes
and the presidents.
His blood started to flow;
his life ebbed away;
his eyes misted over;
his head pained terribly;
his limbs gave way;
his lungs collapsed;
his spirit waned;
        and the crowd was looking on,
        not realizing
        what he had meant
        when he told their wives
        and their daughters:
                "Don't weep for me.
                Weep for yourselves;
                weep for your children."
They did not.
They jeered and they laughed;
they flirted and they danced
while they saw him die
for them,
and because of them.
        The hands of his executioners,
        those of the priests and the kings,
        of the magistrates and their staff,
        were dripping with blood
        because they in the crowd
        kept their hands clean,
        washing themselves free
        from all guilt
        and responsibility,
        like Pilate
        had tried to do,
    ·   in the nightmare
        of the night.

22.

UP WILL PREVAIL

John 20:1–9

Very early in the morning,
as soon as the sun came out,
and as soon as they dared to come out,
they hastened to the tomb.
> The first ones who came
> were the women,
> those who had loved him so very much.
> They were loaded
> with linen,
> oils,
> and perfumes.
> They came to bury him
> properly.
The men
came only afterwards,
when the news
about the empty grave
reached them.
They were running
very fast,
as fast as they could.

John, being the younger,
overtook Peter,
but, being the younger,
he waited for Peter
to enter the tomb.
They all gazed into the tomb
before entering it,
full of hesitation;
they were all surprised,
very surprised.
The story is,
of course,
about what happened
to Jesus,
and yet,
when you read it,
it is
all about them.
First it happened
to Mary;
then it happened
to the other women;
then it happened
to John and Peter;
then to the others,
and finally
to Thomas.
They believed;
they believed:
something had happened
to them.
Something had happened to Jesus,
all right;
that is what we are celebrating today;
correct;
he rose from the dead,
no doubt;
he overcame evil and darkness,
okay;

but the story is really
about what happened to them
when they saw that empty tomb,
when he appeared to them,
a first time,
a second time,
in the house where they met,
outside at the lake,
seeing him walking over the sea,
eating the bread and the fish he fried for them.
The story is about them:
they believed.

> That is how we should
> celebrate this feast;
> what happened to Jesus
> is, of course, the main thing.
> It is the beginning and the end,
> the foundation and the pinnacle,
> but what we are asked to celebrate
> is what overcame them,
> what should overcome us.

What did they believe?
What do they believe
who believe
in the resurrection,
who believe in Jesus?

> Some days ago
> I talked with a very old lady,
> though she herself
> would not like to be called
> that old.
> She told me:
> "As you know,
> life has its
> ups and downs.
> The older you become
> the better you know:
> it is light and darkness,
> sun and shadow,

     sweet and bitter,
     good and evil,
     sickness and health,
     virtue and vice,
     progress and regress,
     falling and rising,
     life and death,
     Good Friday and Easter!"
That is true,
but what they started to believe
at that empty tomb,
what they started to believe
running home,
what they started to believe
seeing him,
what they started to believe
because of him
is:
     that good will overcome,
     that death will disappear,
     that light will triumph,
     that in the end,
     the UP will prevail over the DOWN,
     the UP of the resurrection
     over the DOWN of the cross.
And they were not only willing
to believe,
they were willing
to live that belief
in their lives,
risen themselves
from all death.
Amen.
Alleluia.

23.

UNDOING THE PAST

John 20:19–31

Sitting together
that night,
they did not know
what to hope for.
They wanted him to come,
and they did not want him to come.
  They did want him to come
  to restore their friendship,
  to live in his presence,
  to be energized again by him,
  to hear his voice,
  to see his gestures,
  to touch him,
  to smell him.
They did not want him to come,
not so much
because of him,
but because of what
he would bring
with him:

their recent past,
their cowardice,
their betrayal,
their lack of belief,
their despair,
and their reactions.
Should he come?
Shouldn't he come?
They knew
that the answer
was not theirs,
but his.
They were in doubt;
they were facing a dilemma;
they saw no way out.
And then,
suddenly,
there he stood
in the midst of them.
And again
they did not know
what to do.
Go up to him,
embrace him
as of old,
as if nothing
had happened?
They looked away,
all of them,
their past made them
shy away.
Then he spoke.
He greeted them.
His first word
was:
"Peace;"
And again he said:
"Peace!"

They did not yet dare
to look at his face.
It was clear that
he was forgiving them.
He would not have said
"peace"
if it were not so.
But that peace,
that forgiveness,
was not enough.
Not only he,
but they themselves, too,
were facing their past:
the things they had done,
and the things they had failed
to do.
They had to be able
to forgive themselves,
and the others,
too.

He continued
as if he knew
—and, of course, he knew—
what was bothering them.
While breathing on them
—he was so near
that he was almost,
no,
completely
in the center
of themselves—
he said:
"Whose sins you forgive,
they will be forgiven,
and heaven forgives them,
too."
It was that power
that made them free
from all the past.

They looked at him,
now able to answer
his "peace,"
and they said:
"And with you, too!"
    He had forgiven them;
    they forgave themselves, too.
    The march into the new world
    could start,
    and it did,
    that very evening.
    Amen.

24.

BREAD BROKEN

Luke 24:13-35

Let us first set the scene.
Cleophas and his companion
walked from Jerusalem to Emmaus.
That companion
must have been Cleophas' wife,
otherwise another name
would have been mentioned
in the context of his time.
    According to the experts
    Emmaus was not really a village;
    it was a group of barracks,
    barracks of the Roman Occupational Forces.
    The two, being Jews,
    must have been servants
    in those barracks.
They had taken a weekend off
to go to Jerusalem
to celebrate Passover.
    It is obvious from the story
    that they had heard
    that Jesus had been received as a King

in Jerusalem
the weekend before Passover.
It is also obvious from the story
that Cleophas and his wife
had great hopes.
They had hoped
that Jesus of Nazareth
would manifest himself
as being the Messiah,
changing the whole of their world.
Maybe it had been that hope
that had made them ask
to have the Passover weekend off.
They had hoped
that he would end
their endless struggle
for justice to be done.
They had hoped
that the old glory would be restored to Israel,
and that bread would be shared.

Now they were on their way home;
nothing had happened.
That is to say,
nothing of what they had hoped to happen
had taken place.
All kinds of things had occurred;
events had taken place.
He had been arrested,
tortured,
and crucified.
Maybe they even had seen him
hanging on the cross.
They even knew about the report
that he had risen.
But what they had hoped for
had not taken place;
the Kingdom of God
had not been restored.

Jesus joined them
on the road.
He asked them
why they looked so depressed.
They told him their story.
He explained to them
what had happened.
They listened,
but did they hear?
They heard,
but did they grasp
what they heard?

Arriving at their shelter,
he said that he wanted to go on.
They told him
that he shouldn't do that
because the night was too dark,
and since nothing had changed
as yet
in this world,
there were dangers
everywhere.

He stayed,
and then,
dear friends,
he took *their* bread.
Though being the guest,
and they the hosts,
he took *their* bread,
and broke it.
He gave a piece to her,
and he gave a piece to him.
The sharing had started,
and he disappeared
from their sight.

There they were,
with that piece of bread
in their hands. . . .
They suddenly understood,

they suddenly saw:
it was up to them
from now on.
They rose from their table
—after all
this is a resurrection story—
and they walked
through the night,
now not so dark any more,
to Jerusalem
where the victory had started,
with that bread
in their hearts.
Draw the conclusions
for yourselves.
What are we supposed to do?
We must get things together,
our vision and our techniques,
to take care
that this world is going to be changed
into a place
where bread
is shared
by all.

25.

THE PRICE OF LOVE

John 10:1–10

By comparing himself
to a shepherd,
and us to his sheep,
he is declaring his love
for us.
> Like all such declarations,
> it is a difficult one.
> He is just like us
> in this.
To proclaim one's love
is not only difficult
and delicate,
it has its consequences,
too.
> Love is light,
> love is lighthearted,
> love is joyful,
> love is great,
> love is transcendent,
> love is ecstasy,
> rapture,
> and trance;

love makes you break
through the crust
that keeps you
alone and lonely;
but every love
has a price
that each lover should pay.
I know some people
in a far off town
who picked up neglected children
right from the street,
full of lice,
fleas,
and scabies,
hungry and thirsty,
drugged and underfed,
sick and dirty,
wild and bitter.
They were like sheep,
now together at home,
then scattered again.
Some would return in the evening,
some would not
and had to be looked for
all over the place,
to be found drugged,
arrested,
hit by a car,
or beaten up.
They would get infected
with the most contagious diseases.
They would sell their shirts,
to buy an ice cream,
a cigarette,
a drink,
or pay a girl.
They got lost,
but were found
most of the time.

It was one of the nicest things
those people ever did
—everyone agreed on that—
but also one of the hardest.
Do you understand
what I mean?
Of course
you do.
Didn't you
experience the same?
Parents
love their children
very much;
isn't that the reason that
parents often
suffer
so much?
            "I am the good shepherd,"
            he tells us,
            and he would add
            later on,
            "I am willing to lay down
            my life for you."
That is the price of his love,
the price of ours:
            "Love each other,
            as I have loved you!
            As the Father sent me,
            so I am sending you!"
We should be loving shepherds
to each other,
willing to pay the price.

26.

RESURRECTION AND SOUP

John 14:1–12

We are living
in Easter time.
We are listening
to resurrection stories.
In the second reading of today
we have an unexpected one,
but also a very useful one.
>The reading from the Acts
>is about a scandal,
>a scandal in the early church,
>a scandal in the earliest days.
>It is the scandal of favoritism,
>the scandal of nepotism,
>the scandal of discrimination,
>the scandal of
>—what one would call in Africa—
>brotherization,
>or in South Africa
>*apartheid*.
What happened?

107

It was in Jerusalem,
a town of many widows.
Many of those widows
could not help themselves;
they were poor.
They must have been looking
for a support group.
They found one,
the one offered by the new Christian community,
a community
interested in all.
Everyone in that community believed
that we have the same origin,
the same Father
and the same Mother
in heaven.
>   That community
>   had started a soup-kitchen.
>   Every afternoon
>   the widows came
>   to get their portion.
>   During the first days everything went very well.
>   Everybody was very happy.
But then some of the Hebrew widows
started to profit from the fact
that most community members
were Hebrews.
They asked to be helped first.
They did not come
to the line in the front of the house
any more.
They were helped first
at the back door,
at the kitchen door,
and they got the thickest and the best
part of the soup,
the vegetables,
the barley,
and the beef.

What had started
as a good thing,
as a real manifestation
of what the followers of Jesus Christ
stood for,
had turned into the opposite,
a countersign.
It had become
a scandal.
It was divisive.
It did not only sow hatred,
it broke peace
and it brought war.
Complaints were heard.
They grew louder and louder,
and finally the apostles came together
and they decided
to come to a better work division,
delegating some lay people
to be responsible
for this type of work.
They appointed seven deacons,
ordering them
to be impartial
in the distribution
of the food.
I think
that by now
everyone understands
why this story was told
in resurrection time.
Over there in Jerusalem
they had been caught
in that very old,
and yet so contemporary,
trap
of dividing humanity
according to color,
race, and tribe.

That division
always leads to war
and *death*.
They came out of it.
They rose from that death
remembering
how Jesus had said
that we are brothers and sisters
and having
his attitude
towards all.
That is what they did,
and so should we.

27.

WE WILL HAVE DONE IT

John 14:15–21

There are some experiences
we all have in common.
They are the same
whether we live
in the United States or in Japan,
in China or in East Africa.
> One of those experiences is
> growing up.
> We grew up ourselves,
> I hope;
> we helped others grow up,
> I expect;
> and we have seen others grow up,
> I am sure.
We know the techniques involved;
we know the skills;
we know what should be done.
One example will do.
> We all were brought to school
> up to a certain age,

111

and then our parents decided
that we should do it
on our own.
I remember how I was brought to school,
from home to the school door.
Then one day
my mother said:
"You are big now.
I can't bring you to school
my whole life.
Go on your own.
Tomorrow I won't bring you
any more."
    I still recall
    how proud I was,
    but, at the same time,
    nervous;
    glad,
    and at the same time,
    afraid.
And I went,
but when I reached
the end of the street,
just before going around the corner,
I looked back
and saw my mother
looking through the curtain of a window.
When she saw
that I was looking,
she withdrew.
She did not want me to know
that she, too,
was proud and nervous,
glad and afraid.
    Jesus had been with them
    for so long.
    He had done so much for them:
    every time they were hungry,
    there had been food;

every time they were thirsty,
there had been fine wine;
every time they were sick,
he had healed them;
every time they were in debt,
he had bailed them out.
True,
he had been sending them out,
but they had always been able
to come back,
to sit down at his feet,
to listen to his counsel,
to profit from his presence.
They were quite responsible persons,
fathers and mothers of families,
professionals,
but in a way,
they had become too dependent,
like children,
like teenagers,
following their leader
in all things.

He spoke to them,
and he said:
"A little while,
and I will be with you
no longer;
a little while,
and you will be alone;
a little while,
and you will be independent;
a little while,
and you will have to stand
on your own feet,
and no longer
on mine."
When he saw their frightened faces,
when he saw the growing despair in their eyes,
he added:

"But I won't leave you alone.
Another helper will be given to you:
a helper from within,
a helper from within you,
the *Holy Spirit.*
He will help you
in everything;
she will help you
from within;
he will help you to do,
all I did for you,
and even greater things."
He asked us
to walk
on our own,
in his direction.
He asked us
to do
what he had told us to do
in such a way
that in the end
we would be able to say:
"It is we who did it
with Him,
that is true,
but it was WE. . . .

28.

AND MARY THE MOTHER OF JESUS

John 17:1–11

This Sunday
is an in-between Sunday,
a Sunday of waiting:
waiting for Pentecost.
> His disciples were doing the same
> in the first reading of today.
> They had locked themselves up,
> together with their wives
> (and their children, of course),
> in that room,
> out of fear.
Mary was with them.
It is the last time
that she is mentioned
in Holy Scripture,
the last time
that a role is given to her.
> They were praying,
> but they had no "spirit" at all.
> They were praying,

115

but what were they praying for?
What did they think would happen?
Nobody knows.
The doors were closed,
the windows, too.
Now and then
one of them would slip
in or out
to get some food,
but that was all.
They had no spirit,
no life.
No anything.
It happened to me
so very often in East Africa,
over all the years
that I had the privilege of living there,
that theological associations
in high schools and colleges
would ask me to give talks to them.
I gave so many talks
that in the end
I could guess
—more or less—
what questions to expect
at question time.
A youngster would stand up,
raise her hand
—it was almost always
a she—
and say:
"Sir,"
because that is what they called me,
"Sir,
how is it
that we hear about miracles and conversions
in Jesus' time
how is it
that we hear about all kinds of wonderful things
in the early days of the church,

while now,
among us
in these, our days,
nothing ever seems to happen?"
And all the others
in the hall
would applaud
and shout:
"Point, point,
she has a point!"
to tell me,
that it was their question,
too.
          Isn't it a question
          of all of us?
          Why is the church so dead
          nowadays?
          Why does nothing,
          nothing ever happen?
In the end,
I had an answer
ready.
And I often used
the first reading of today,
pointing out
that once
in the early church
there was a time, too,
when nothing seemed to happen
either,
in those days
before Pentecost:
          they were afraid,
          they were disappointed,
          they were frustrated,
          they were cold,
          they were hopeless,
          they were locked in,
          they were waiting,
          they wanted to run away,

and in fact,
they would have run away,
I think,
if Mary
had not been there.
She kept them together.
She called them back from the door
when they wanted to sneak out
with their wives and their children.
She said:
"Wait,
and pray,
and one day
his promises
will be fulfilled.
Wait and the Spirit will come
alive in you."
And they listened,
and they waited
till the Spirit
came.

It was not only in those days
that Mary played that role.
She has been doing that
all through human history.
At the moment that the church
had cooled down
below a spiritual freezing point,
she often would appear,
playing that role.
When midway through the last century,
France had cooled down
to the point
that all life in the church seemed dead,
that no signs of the presence of the Holy Spirit
were given anymore,
she appeared in Lourdes
and immediately
there were signs galore of that Spirit:

miracles and conversions,
renewed prayer,
and even a new source of water
that started to stream
to the amazement of all.
>Wasn't it the same
>in Portugal,
>when she appeared in Fatima?
And what about her appearance
in Guadalupe
many more years ago.
Did you ever hear
about the role she played there?
>The last remark about Mary
>in the Bible is:
>*"They were in the company of Mary."*
>A last remark:
>nothing has changed
>since then.

29.

THE SHIFT IN THEM

John 20:19–23

That day their spirit changed.
That is clear from all the reports
that reached us,
spanning two-thousand years.
What happened to them?
Did anything like it ever happen to us?
    Let us try to understand.
    Just consider:
    you wrote a letter
    to someone you love.
    He left for another place
    and is very far away.
    You are waiting for an answer,
    two days,
    three days,
    four days.
    By now the answer should have come,
    but it has not come.
    One week,
    two weeks,
    three weeks go by,

and you start to worry
about the letter
you wrote.
Did you write anything
that could have been misunderstood?
Did you write anything wrong?
You try to remember what you wrote.
You curse yourself
because you did not make a copy.
    And no answer comes.
    What could it have been?
    You are getting scared.
    Did you lose her
    for the rest of your life?
    Will you never hear from him
    again?
    You hardly sleep any more.
    The worry shows in your face.
    It might be totally over;
    it might be finished;
    and all the plans you made together
    might be for nought.
    People around you
    start to ask you
    what is wrong.
And then one day
the telephone rings,
and there is your friend,
and she says:
"Hi, how are you?
Glad to hear your voice.
Peace, peace!"
    And your whole mind shifts.
    Your whole spirit changes
    from fear to joy,
    an enormous joy.
    What a relief!
And now think of his disciples
and what they had done to him.

They had dreamed together;
they had talked together;
they had loved each other;
they had planned together
what they were going to do
in order to change this whole world,
to build a road
to the nicest star,
a human city of justice and peace.
> But then,
> suddenly,
> all had gone awry.
> He had been arrested;
> he had been beaten up;
> he had been crucified;
> and they had run away
> like frightened chickens,
> all of them.
> They had just left him alone.
> It was not only Peter who had betrayed him,
> nor Judas,
> > but all of them.
They had heard
that he had appeared to women,
some of his friends.
They had told them
that he had risen.
But he had not appeared to them,
his disciples.
> To others: yes.
> To them: no.
They were sitting together,
complaining about each other to each other:
if only we had done this,
if only we had not said that,
why have we been so stupid,
would he ever forgive,
would he ever want to be with them again,
would he ever let them join
in the bringing of the Kingdom of God?

They talked like people do
after the death of someone they love:
if only . . .
if only. . . .
And while they were talking like that,
he suddenly appeared.
They were scared stiff.
What was he going to do:
scold them,
chase them away,
punish them,
leave them,
annihilate them?
> He did not.
> He did not do anything like that at all.
> He greeted them,
> and he said:
> "Peace,
> peace be with you!"
"What did he say?"
"Did he say peace?"
"Yes, he said peace."
So all is good;
all is well;
so it will go on;
so we still will be in;
oh yes,
of course.
> It was in that way,
> that something changed
> in their minds.
> It was in that way
> that somethng shifted
> in their spirit:
> they were suddenly
> full.
> They were suddenly filled
> with SPIRIT,
> full,
> totally full.

They knew:
there will be peace
between him and us.
They knew:
there will be peace
between us and them.
They knew:
there will be a solution
to all our human problems,
the hunger and the thirst,
the injustice and discrimination,
the laziness and irresponsibility.
> That is how we should be filled,
> today,
> and all the days of our lives.
Together,
we will be together with him.

30.

EMPOWERMENT

John 3:16–18

A preacher is often tempted,
especially on a day like this
when the theme is Trinity,
to try to say it all,
to try to say too much.
> To say it all
> is impossible;
> to try to say too much
> is at the end,
> sometimes for the second half,
> and in certain cases
> from the very beginning,
> very boring.
So I will be saying only a little,
giving, I hope, some idea,
some inspiration,
that might be useful on the occasion
of this celebration.
> Something that is neither a mere repetition
> of things we have heard over and over before,

nor something that is completely new,
and therefore unrecognizable.
Something that helps us along,
something that helps us forward.
An idea that makes us shift a bit
what we believe,
what we hope,
and what we love.
A small modulation
that, nevertheless,
will help us all
to find some new enthusiasm,
and that will help all those around us,
too.
That is why I would like
to see us believe in the Trinity,
that we just heard described by Paul,
in a new kind of way,
in a new light,
so that even his command
to go and teach,
and baptize them
in the name of the Father,
and the Son,
and the Holy Spirit,
might light up again in us
with a new brightness.
Let me start with an experience
that is very significant for me.
I had this experience in Africa,
an experience of people
who very often said of themselves,
when confronted with alien cultures,
that they felt in these new strange cultures,
powerless,
frustrated,
and diminished;
that they felt like nobodies,
unimportant and useless.

You can have,
here in this country,
here in this town,
those feelings, too.
I am sure of that.
I heard them.
I saw them.
I met them.
And I smelled them.
     At one time or another,
     all of us
     can be struck by that type of feeling
     when we read of the developments
     all around us.
It is rather obvious
from the reports on him
that when God's son,
Jesus Christ,
moved through this time,
moved through this space,
he had the same kind of experience:
     day and night,
     he was surrounded by people
     who were blind,
     who were deaf,
     who were paralyzed,
     who were mute,
     who were afraid,
     who in their own eyes
     could hardly do anything at all,
     paralyzed like flies
     in the web of the intriguing spiders
     around them,
     cocooned by political and religious
     ropes, strings, straps,
     shackles, fetters, and manacles.
And you know
what the Son of God and the Son of Man
did to them.

He always did the same:
    the blind saw,
    the deaf heard
    the paralyzed walked,
    the mute spoke,
    those afraid got courage,
    and those who had been hardly anything at all
    in their own eyes
    were liberated
    and became prime movers
    in the history of salvation
    he started among us.
They said:
"There are no fish.
What are we to do?"
He said:
"There are fish.
You, throw out your net.
I will make you
fishers of men."
    They said:
    "There is no bread.
    What are we going to give them to eat?"
    He said:
    "You divide what you have.
    There is plenty for all."
They said:
"We cannot pray."
He said:
"Start praying like this:
Our Father. . . . "
And they who had thought that they could not pray,
did pray after that.
    In modern American a word is used
    to indicate the strategy he applied.
    The word is
    empower.
    He empowered them.

And that is what he asked his disciples to do
when he sent them out saying:
>   baptize them
>   in the power they have,
>   the power of their origin,
>   created by the Father;
>   the power of their kinship,
>   blood-related to Jesus Christ the Son;
>   the power of the Holy Spirit
>   in them.

That is the reality
I would like us to meditate upon,
hoping that it may cause in us,
in our hearts and in our minds,
that little shift
that might make
all the difference
in our lives,
and in what we believe
to be our mission
in his name.

>   Do we feel empowered by him,
>   in the name of the Father,
>   the Son,
>   and the Holy Spirit?
>   Are we, because of that empowerment,
>   living and acting in such a way,
>   that those around us,
>   maybe blind, deaf, dumb,
>   diminished and frustrated
>   in their own eyes,
>   are empowered,
>   too?

31.

BODY OF CHRIST

John 6:51–58

The feast we celebrate today
is called
Corpus Christi:
the Body of Christ.
    After having celebrated
    the Holy Spirit on Pentecost
    and the Trinity on Trinity Sunday,
    we are invited to come back
    to that other dimension
    in him,
    to that other dimension
    in us,
    body,
    matter
    —a matter
    that matters,
    very much.
We are of one Spirit,
we are of his Spirit.
We are of one Body,
we are his Body.

You can see that,
and experience it,
when you look again
at what happened
that evening
when he took
the bread,
when he took
the wine,
and said
—*while sharing that bread,*
while sharing that wine—
    "This is my body,
    this is my blood!"
When he was holding up
that "bread" and that "wine,"
it was His Body,
it was His Blood.
It was our Body,
it was Our Blood,
when they shared
that "bread" and that "wine."
Some days ago I was in Washington DC,
in the National Shrine.
A dozen or so pilgrims
came out of the grandiose basilica.
They had just participated in a Mass.
They had just received Holy Communion,
communion with Him,
communion in Him
with each other,
forming together with him
his Body, his Blood.
I saw them;
I even saw
that a blind man
received communion
with them.
    They came out of church
    together with him.

He walked among them,
tapping the pavement
in front of him
with his cane.
He did not see them,
being blind,
but he must have been aware of them,
all talking excitedly,
feeling a bit lost
in a strange town.
They did not see him either,
though they were not blind.
They were too busy with themselves.
He ended up in the midst of them.
Someone stepped on his cane,
bending it,
while he was pushed on.
And even then
they did not see him.
They left him alone
trying to straighten his cane.

> They all had been to communion
> together,
> in Jesus,
> who said
> of all of them:
> "This is my body,
> this is my blood!"

Yet,
when it came
to everyday life,
that reality got lost,
the body
did not seem to have formed.
They were not really in communion.
They did not really form
his Body,
our Body,
did they?
Do we?

32.

PETER AND PAUL

Matthew 16:13–19

Peter and Paul
did not have very much in common
before they met Jesus.
Peter was a very simple,
uneducated
fisherman;
Paul was a highly-qualified
very educated
scholar.
One thing, however,
they did have in common
before they met Jesus.
> Both of them
> were living
> in a very small
> and closed
> world.
> Both of them
> were living
> in a very small
> and closed
> circle.

Their circles and their worlds
were different,
but they were equally restrictive.
> Peter's world
> was his family
> and his small boat
> on not too large a lake.
> Paul's world
> was his study,
> with all the books
> and the scrolls,
> he had read
> over and over again.
Being narrow-minded,
they did not like change.
They hated it.
You can notice that
in the reports on them.
> When Paul first heard
> about the Christians,
> he saw them as a threat
> to his world,
> and he simply decided
> to terminate them all.
> When Peter heard
> that Paul wanted to introduce
> non-Jews into the community,
> he objected;
> he saw them as a threat
> to his world,
> and he simply decided,
> not to accept them at all.
Neither of the two
was very daring,
neither of the two
was very courageous.
If they had not met Christ,
we would not have heard of them
at all.

They both would have died
like shy mice
in their holes:
>Peter very quietly in bed,
>smelling of fish;
>Paul very quietly in his study
>smelling of paper and ink.

It was their contact with Jesus
that opened up their world,
that make them break through
their circles.
>It was Jesus who told them
>that God was the Father,
>and the Universe the Mother of all,
>that with him as our brother,
>we should form
>the one family of God,
>and that only in that way,
>would we come
>to fulfillment and salvation.

With that idea in their heads,
with that ideal in their hearts,
they started to travel
all through the world
bringing that news around,
risking their lives
on land and on sea,
and even
>—when Paul descended
>in a basket
>over a town wall
>to escape from arrest—

in the air.
>They knew that these ideas
>did not come from them.
>They knew themselves to be too narrow-minded.
>They knew that these ideals
>came from God,
>and believing that,

    they found the courage
    to break through the small worlds
    in which they lived,
    preaching all over the world,
    thinking not only of themselves,
    their families and their success,
    their food and their drink,
    their sports and their leisure,
    but interested in all,
    in the kingdom of God.
Let us pray
that we may pick up
something of their wideness of vision,
of their belief,
their hope,
and their love.
Amen.

33.

REVEALED TO THE MEREST CHILDREN

Matthew 11:25-30

Very many children,
I think all children,
love to listen to stories,
to fairy tales,
to those very old fairy tales.
They love them especially
before they go to bed,
before they fall asleep.
> They will ask you
> —if you give them a chance—
> "Dad, Mom, Grandma,
> please tell me a story,
> a fairy tale!"
> And you sit on their bed,
> and they plant their thumbs
> firmly in their mouths,
> ready to listen.
> Their cheeks are already very pink
> and their ears glow
> because they are almost asleep,

137

but they want to hear that story,
the story in which a bad stepmother
changes into a good one,
a story in which a dragon is killed,
a story in which lost children find their home,
a story in which the princess wakes up
from a very long sleep.
In all those tales,
dangers are overcome,
evil is undone,
fear is chased away,
sadness disappears,
darkness is lit up,
flowers start to bloom,
the sun shines,
the bride kisses the groom,
and they live happily
ever after. . . .
It is not difficult to guess
why children like those stories.
Their day is over,
they are going to sleep,
a lot of unpleasant things have happened to them.
They heard so often
"Don't do this,
do that!
Stop talking,
say something!"
that they got very confused,
and very upset.
And that is why,
before falling asleep
they like to hear
the happy end
to the story you tell.
One day
my prince,
or my princess,
will come;

and with that idea in mind,
they fall asleep
and off they go
to the land of dreams.
>   And if you changed the story,
>   if the bad stepmother won
>   if the dragon ate the prince,
>   if the children did not find their home,
>   if the princess did not wake up,
>   a thumb would come out of that mouth,
>   and you would be told:
>   "Wrong,
>   you are telling it all wrong.
>   It is not like that.
>   Start again!"

The first reading of today
is such a fairy tale.
It is about a king
who enters his kingdom
sitting on a donkey;
and the king sitting on the back
of that animal
is going to do something:
he is going to banish
all war-chariots,
he is going to banish
all war-horses,
he is going to banish
all weapons,
all arrows and bows.
>   The chariots of that time
>   are the tanks and armored cars of our days;
>   the horses of those days
>   are the jet fighters of our time;
>   those arrows and bows
>   are our missiles and their launching pads.

He is going to undo all that.
He is going to destroy them once and for all,
and there will be peace among the nations.

There will be peace from sea to sea,
from the river to the ends of the earth.

    I am sure
    that very many of us will say:
    "Very nice,
    very beautiful,
    but it is only a story,
    a fairy tale,
    a story for the children,
    a story for the birds.
    Don't be silly,
    don't be naive.
    Let us be sensible.
    A thing like that
    will never ever happen.
    Humanity will
    never,
    never
    change!"

        And they bang their chests,
        and they wink an eye,
        and they don't even want
        to hear about it
        any more.

Yes,
it is a story,
but from the Old Testament,
not a fairy tale
but a prophecy.
And it is of this type of tale
that Jesus said
in the gospel of today:

    "Father, Lord of heaven and earth,
    to you I offer praise,
    for what you have hidden
    from the learned and the clever,
    you have revealed to the merest children.
    Father, it is true!"
    Amen.

34.

LOST ALONGSIDE THE ROAD

Matthew 13:1-23

The gospel of today
is a complaint,
a serious complaint
directed to us:
>God's word
>often falls dead
>on its soil.
>It is trampled,
>it is drying up,
>it is drowned,
>it does not grow.
The signs God gives
in our lives
remain unseen,
>unheard,
>unfelt,
>untouched
>and powerless.
I am sure
that it has happened to you,

that a sign
you wanted to give
to another
got lost.

> There was a young man,
> who had a misunderstanding
> with his girlfriend,
> a very serious misunderstanding.
> He was upset about it
> because it spoiled their relationship
> entirely,
> and he liked her very much.

He tried to talk to her,
but it did not work.
He tried to phone her,
but at the moment he heard her voice,
he did not know what to say,
and he had to hang up.
He tried to write her a letter,
but when he finished,
he tore his letter up
because he thought
it sounded too silly.

> Then he remembered
> that she liked roses,
> dark red roses.
> He bought her a rose,
> only one
> because roses were very expensive
> that time of the year.
> The man in the flowershop
> put some ferns with the rose,
> and wrapped it in some nice, thin paper.

The young man went to her apartment,
and put the rose down
in front of her door
at the time
he knew
she would come home.

He himself hid
around the corner
behind some trashcans.
    Then she came,
    lovely as ever.
    His heart bounced
    in his throat;
    his mouth suddenly got dry,
    very dry.
She opened her purse
and took out her key.
She opened the door
and stepped inside
without having noticed
his lovely, beautiful, expensive rose
at all.
    What a disappointment,
    what a horror,
    what a tragedy,
    what a missed chance.
It is in those terms
that John,
that God,
speaks to us.
    God gives us signs
    day after day
    to draw our attention:
        a flower,
        a thought,
        a dream,
        a child,
        a person,
        a fine feeling,
        sometimes even a pain.
    How often
    do we notice?
    How often
    do we stop and say:
    "Hello,

> thank you,
> my God"?

We live
as those who have eyes,
but do not see;
as those who have ears,
but do not hear;
not only as far as God is concerned,
but even as far as the people
around us are concerned.

> Is it not exactly
> through them
> that God
> so often
> tries to speak
> to us?

Isn't that
what God tried to do
through Jesus?

35.

LETTING GROW

Matthew 13:24–43

The disciples around him
were very clear
—they thought—
on good and evil,
on blessings and curses,
on virtue and vice,
on wheat and weed;
but they were not farmers,
not even one of them,
as far as we know.
>Most of them
>were fishermen,
>who immediately after a haul
>pulled in their nets
>and assorted their catch:
>>the good ones,
>>the edible and marketable ones
>>*here*,
>>and the bad ones,
>>the unedible and poisonous ones
>>*there*.

145

"Lord,"
they said,
"Lord,
can't you destroy the evil?
Can't you do away with the bad
once and for all,
like we do
on the beach,
so that only
goodness and sweetness
are left?"

     He was not a farmer either,
     but his heavenly Father
     was,
     as he himself had said.
     He knew about a field,
     He knew about that field of his Father,
     the field called *world*
     and he said:
     "You can't do that.
     You can't use your fishermen's tactics
     in the *shamba** of this world.
     It you did that,
     if you tried to separate
     the good and the bad,
     radically like that,
     you would spoil it all.
     The two are so closely intertwined,
     so radically in their roots,
     that pulling up one
     means
     pulling up the other.
     Let them both grow,
     trusting in God.
     Didn't the Father sow
     the seed that is good?
     Was it not the devil
     who sowed the seed
     that is bad?

Goodness will win,
light will conquer darkness.
Don't be afraid!"
We live in a time
that he is surrounded,
again,
by disciples
who know very well
—they think—
what is good
and what is bad,
what is just
and what is unjust,
what is weed
and what is wheat.
There is nothing wrong in that.
On the contrary,
we wish
that everyone knew it
as well
as they do.
Demonstrations and protest marches,
sit-ins and strikes
galore.
But again
they seem to be
like those fishermen
who say:
"Can't we throw the good ones
here
and the bad ones
there?"
They forget
that just like in a field
—didn't he call us
God's acre?—
goodness and badness,
justice and injustice,
blessing and curse,

are so radically intertwined in us
as persons
that rooting up one
makes the rest fall.
He said:
"Don't do that.
Let them both grow,
but do take care
that goodness wins.
I am all for that,
until
the end."

---

*Shamba: Kiswahili for field.

36.

THE TREASURE IN YOU

Matthew 13:44–52

I would like to tell you a story.
It is an old story.
It is a well-known story.
It is your story.
It is my story,
at least it might be.
Maybe it should be.
> There was a man
> who had a dream
> one night.
> He dreamed how he left his house,
> his hearth,
> his cooking stones,
> his cooking pot,
> his wife,
> and his children,
> and walked,
> walked,
> and walked.
> He passed one village
> after another,

and he finally came to a place
with a bridge in the road,
just before the entrance to a village.
He dreamed
that he started to dig
under that bridge,
and that he found
under that bridge
a real treasure.
When he woke up,
he did not pay any attention
to his dream.
But then, a second night,
     a third night,
     a fourth night,
     a fifth night,
     a sixth night,
     a seventh night,
he had that same dream.
So he said to himself:
This must be true.
I must find that bridge,
I must find that village,
I must find that treasure.
He left his wife,
and he left his children,
and he left his cooking stones,
and he left his cooking pot,
and he left his hearth,
and he started to walk,
he passed village,
after village, after village,
until he arrived at a place
with a bridge in the road,
just before the entrance to the village.
He recognized the place immediately.
He was overjoyed.
He went from the road
down under the bridge

and started to dig.
He dug, and he dug,
but he found nothing.
Then an old woman came along.
She stopped, and asked him:
"What are you doing there?"
And he asked her,
"Why do you want to know?"
And she told him
how she had had a dream,
night after night
over the last seven nights,
and in that dream she had seen a man
digging for treasure
and she had dreamed
that she had said to that man:
"What you are looking for
you can only find at your home.
It is under your own hearth,
    under your own cooking pot,
    under your own three cooking stones."
When the man heard this,
he stopped digging
and he went home,
running as fast as he could.
And when he arrived home
in the midst of his wife and his children,
he started to dig
under his own fireplace,
under his own cooking stones,
under his own cooking pot.
They helped him,
all of them.
And there,
lo and behold,
he found his treasure,
and he was very happy
ever after,
together with them.

In the gospel of today,
Jesus invites us
to look for our treasure,
to look for a pearl,
to look for the Kingdom of God,
but he tells us also
where we should look for it.
He said:
"The Kindom of God,
God's power and love,
God's mercy and energy,
God's light and God's life
is *WITHIN* you."
Sisters and brothers,
dear friends,
may I ask you
to look for your treasure,
to look for your pearl,
to look for your life,
within you,
within your relationships?
Open your heart,
open your mind,
and you will be
like that householder,
who took from his own stock,
old
and
new,
to feed and help
those around him.

37.

WHAT WOULD JESUS HAVE DONE?

Matthew 14:13-21

It was somewhere in a small,
but not too small, village.
A stranger had arrived;
he had come from very far.
You could easily see that;
he was dressed in a strange way,
he was very dusty,
and no one could understand
what he was saying.

     Just as he entered the village,
     something terrible happened to him.
     A car hit him from behind;
     he fell over,
     and started to bleed from his mouth,
     and even from his ears.
     But the car passed on
     after the accident.
     The man crept
     with great difficulty
     into the shade of a tree.

Some villagers stopped
to have a look at him,
but they all walked on,
seeing that they had no way
of communicating with him
at all.

Some of those villagers happened to be Christians.
They, too, looked at him,
and his blood and his misery,
but they, too, passed on,
though some of them
discussed
what Jesus would have done.
"Of course,"
they said,
"Jesus would have helped him.
If only Jesus were here,
that man would be helped.
What a pity
that Jesus is not here."
And they looked at each other,
and they looked once more at that man
who just whimpered,
very softly,
"Help,"
in that language
nobody understood.
If only Jesus
were here!
A strange story,
isn't it?

That evening
they were hungry,
very hungry.
They had followed him
for too long.
They were not able to walk home
with their old people and their children
without getting into serious difficulties.
The first ones had fainted already.

He saw them,
and he took whatever bread and fish
he could find,
and helped them.
Of course,
he was Jesus.
> At the moment it is
> evening,
> almost night,
> in many countries in Africa.
> In twenty-four countries,
> there are regions with starving people.
> One hundred fifty million people might be affected
> by famine
> over the coming years.
> That starvation is not only due
> to the drought.
> It is due to all kinds of causes
> that started long before the drought:
> wrong agricultural policies,
> unjust land division,
> too much outside
> and inside interest in nonedible cashcrops,
> the neglect of means of transport and warehousing,
> unequal distribution of food,
> exaggerated and inflated prices for fertilizers,
> too low prices paid to the farmers,
> and so on.

What would Jesus have done?
He would have helped, of course.
All over the world
Christians and others
are doing that,
giving and lobbying for food-aid.
> That aid will come too late
> for many;
> that aid cannot help
> ultimately,
> that aid is no solution
> to the real problems.

> To solve those problems,
> much has to be done
> in Africa,
> and all of us
> live under the obligation
> of doing that,
> wherever we are,
> wherever we have an influence,
> by our decisions
> or by our work.

The first problem
that the first Christian community
solved in Jerusalem
so long ago
was the problem
of the distribution of food,
so that everyone would have sufficient,
and nobody would be short.

> It is true
> that Jesus will help us.
> What Isaiah said is true:
> that God will give us plenty,
> God will do that,
> but
> *through us.*

The story in the beginning
was not ended.
Some people of the Mothers' Union
of the local Christian community,
heard about that man.
They went to dress his wounds,
and they gave his something to eat and drink.
While they were doing that,
they thought
that they heard
the wounded man say:
"True religion!"
He met
at that moment
Jesus in them.

38.

PRAYING AND LISTENING

Matthew 14:22–33

He went up on the mountain
by himself to pray.
> There was a man,
> a very old man.
> He had children,
> he had grandchildren,
> he had uncles,
> he had aunts,
> he had brothers,
> he had sisters,
> and yet, he was very lonely
> because no one in the family
> ever sat down
> to talk with him.

They gave him food,
they gave him drink,
they gave him clothing,
they brought him to bed,
they got him out of bed,
but every time
he said:

"I would like to talk to you,"
they hurried away
and they answered:
"Sorry, I have no time,"
or
"Sorry, I am in a hurry,"
because they knew
that if they listened,
he might ask them
to do something for him,
that if they listened,
he might trouble them.

    I think that all of us
    know such a man,
    know such a woman,
    we would not like
    to sit down with
    to talk things over,
    because if we do,
    our lives might get too complicated.
    We might get too involved.
And that is why
so many of us
feel lonely
and desperate.

    God must be like that, too.
    God wants to say so very much to us.
    God would like us to change our world,
    I am sure.
    We know that all too well.
    That is why
    we do not like to listen
    to God;
    that is why we do not like to do
    what Jesus did,
    what that prophet Elijah did.
We do not like to sit down
calmly,
in a cave,

or on a mountain top,
in our room,
in a church
or in a chapel,
to listen
to what God might say
about us
to us.
    The man
    who drinks too much
    does not want to listen;
    the woman
    who neglects her children
    does not want to listen;
    the teacher
    who does not teach
    does not want to listen;
    the thief
    who steals
    does not want to listen.
    They all know
    that if they do,
    if they sit down,
    if they listen,
    if they pray,
    God will tell them,
    in the deepest part of their person,
    that they should not drink,
    that they should not neglect their children,
    that they should teach,
    and that they should not steal.
We do not mind
coming to Mass
to sing hymns,
to organize celebrations,
putting on our Sunday best,
giving offerings.
    But to sit down
    and to listen to God,

in the quiet of the evening
on a mountaintop,
or in our room,
as Jesus did,
that is too dangerous,
that is too hazardous.
Just think of what God,
might ask us to do.
Yet,
it is what all prophets did,
what all saints did,
what Jesus did,
what Peter did,
when God said:
"May I come to you?"
It is
what we should do,
and just like them,
we will be asked,
like they all were,
to help
in the changing of this world,
and of our own minds and hearts.

39.

NO STRANGER

Matthew 15:21–28

Jesus was traveling
in a pagan region,
a non-Jewish region.
He himself said
that he had not come
for the pagans,
but only for the Jews.
His disciples went further than that.
According to them,
pagans were no good,
there was only evil
in them.

> What happened to them
> in that strange country
> remains strange, too.
> Did he want to tell them
> that they were wrong?
> Maybe.
> They definitely did not like
> that alien woman
> shouting after them.

The whole episode
reminds me of another story
told to me by an Irish sister
living in a hospital in Nairobi,
the capital of Kenya.
For quite some time
that hospital had no residential doctor,
and that is why it was closed
during the night.
There were other hospitals in town
with 24-hour service,
but this hospital did not have that.

    It happened one night
    that a ten-year-old child
    living near the hospital
    got very sick.
    She started to shake,
    to weep,
    to cry,
    to whimper.
    Her mother did not know what to do,
    and in her panic she forgot
    that the hospital near by
    was closed.
    So she went to it
    with her child.
    At the hospital the doors were closed.
    There was no light,
    everyone was asleep,
    nobody heard her.
    She shouted,
    she knocked on the doors,
    she rattled the gates,
    all to no avail.
    It remained dark.
She went home with her child
who got more and more upset.
She even had to carry her;
all the color had drained from her face.

Coming home she wanted to ask help
from her neighbors.
But it was dark everywhere.
She knocked on some doors,
but she was not heard,
or, maybe, they were too afraid to open the door
in the middle of the night.
    Then she saw a light
    in a house at the end of the street.
    It was the house of someone she did not know,
    a Muslim family.
    The lights were still on
    because they were celebrating their fast
    ramadan
    when Muslims only eat something
    during the night.
She never had contacted them,
she hardly ever greeted them,
she considered them pagans,
strangers,
but it was the only light
in the dark of that
night.
    She went to the house;
    she knocked on the door;
    a lady opened the door,
    her head covered in a veil.
    She explained her case,
    and the woman said,
    looking at the whimpering child,
    "My husband is not at home;
    he is celebrating *ramadan* with some friends,
    and I have no driver's license.
    Have you one?"
    She answered:
    "Yes, I have!"
    and the Muslim lady went into the house,
    and gave her
    —a total stranger—

her car-key
in the middle of that night,
in an African country,
where a car
is a hundred times more precious
than in America.
She took the car,
her child was admitted,
and when she told the story to that sister
the next day
she said:
"I never saw a mercy
and a faith
like that.
She was so good,
so full of God's mercy.
She heard all my prayers
that night!"
Jesus was standing in their midst,
they all despised that Canaanite woman,
they had told him already:
"Let us get rid of her!"
But he listened to her,
and after she spoke,
he said to them:
"Did you hear that?
There is faith in her,
she believes in me,
she believes in God's promises,
she is full of hope,
she has a faith
greater than yours,
she,
this stranger."
It is what he still wants to tell us,
there is good in the others,
they are not all bad,
though they might organize things
in a way different from ours.

Isaiah said it
in the first reading of today:
all people of good will
are marching
in the direction of God
with the obvious consequence
that they are marching in a way
that they are going to meet each other.
This should not only be
a theoretical thought;
it should lead
to practical conclusions.
We should live this belief
in respect and in love,
willing to allow
others to grow
in the goodness
and the godliness
they have in common with us,
in this *network*
that spans
the whole of humanity,
past, present, and future.

40.

DIVINITY IN ALL OF US

Matthew 16:13–20

They were surrounding him,
simple people,
his disciples,
fishermen,
people who did not think very much
of themselves.
People nobody thought very much
of either.
Nobody had ever asked for their opinions,
nobody had ever paid any attention to
what they thought
or felt.
> The people who mattered
> looked down upon them.
> They smelled of fish.
> The smell came out of their hair
> and out of their clothing.
And now he
whom they followed as their model,
whom they imitated like children,
whom they were surprised
to be allowed to follow,

now he
asked them:
    "What name
    would you give me?
    Whom do you,
    people,
    say that I am?"
They could not believe their ears.
It was impossible that he was asking
for their opinions.
That is why they started by telling him
what the scribes,
what the priests,
what the Pharisees,
what the political leaders,
what the important ones
were saying;
and they answered:
    "They,
    those other ones,
    say
    that you are
        John the Baptist;
    others say:
        Jeremiah,
    others:
        Elijah,
    and again others:
        one of the prophets.
Then he said,
"But you,
whom do you say I am?"
They looked at each other:
was he really going to pay attention
to what they thought?
Again they looked at each other;
they nudged at Peter,
obviously their leader,
and he said:

"I know who you are,
we know who you are.
You are the Messiah,
you are the Son of God."
> And then Jesus said something strange.
> He said:
> "Peter,
> how blessed are you
> because you do not say that of yourself.
> What you said
> came from God,
> God in you."
Sister or brother,
what Jesus said of Peter
he also said of us.
Don't we believe
that Jesus is the Messiah?
Don't we believe
that Jesus is the Son of God?
Isn't that the reason
that we came together
here today?
> *That same God the Father*
> *who was in Peter*
> *must be in us.*
We are charged
with the Father's Spirit;
we are full of the Son's Spirit;
God is in us.
> I invite you
> to stand in front of your mirror
> once you are home again
> and, looking at yourself,
> you should say:
> "Look at him,
> look at her,
> *charged with God,*
> *full of Spirit.*"
We often think of ourselves
as totally negative,

as non-participants
in so many affairs,
in a sense good-for-nothings,
just like his disciples did.
  Others are important,
  others lead the world.
We forget
the good in us,
God in us.
We overlook our potentialities,
our dignity,
our access
to life itself.
  I met an African bishop
  who some years ago
  was described
  as a contemporary saint
  by the weekly magazine *TIME*:
  Bishop Christopher Mwoleka
  from Rulenge in Tanzania.
He said that
we need two types of confessional boxes
in our churches,
some at the right side,
and some at the left side.
  In the left ones,
  you confess your sins,
  getting as a penance
  going to the ones on the right side,
  with the obligation
  to confess honestly
  the good you did,
  the good in you,
  God in you.
That is what Jesus said of Peter:
blessed are you, Peter,
God is with you.
Amen

41.

TO SPREAD OUR ARMS

Matthew 16:21-27

A story is only interesting
when it is recognizable.
If there is nothing in a story
that reminds us of something that happened,
or might have happened,
to us,
it is irrelevant.
It is very difficult
to listen to those stories.
Very quickly we give up,
and we fall asleep.
> That is why it is so difficult
> for young people
> to listen to the stories
> about the old days.
> They can't imagine
> the things that happened then,
> and the circumstances people lived under.
> That is why it is so difficult
> for old people
> to listen to the experiences
> of the young.

They don't even know
what they are talking about.
When I tell you
that in Africa
women and children
have to walk every day
for two, three, or even more hours
to fetch the water
they need
for one or two days,
you don't know what I am talking about,
because you have a tap
in your bathroom and in your kitchen
that gives water
when and where
and as much as you want.
When I tell you about hunger,
how at the moment
very many people are on the point of dying
from starvation,
how would you be able to understand,
surrounded as you are,
by shops and supermarkets?
It is the same with the stories
in the gospel.
It is the same with the gospel story
of today.
If there were nothing in that tale
that reminded us
of something that happened to us
during our life,
it would remain irrelevant,
boring, and uninteresting.
But I think
that what happened to Jesus
is recognizable
from within our own lives.
What happened?
He had decided to go on with his mission. .

He had decided to go on giving himself
in view of the others,
healing them,
teaching them,
taking care of them,
bringing them to themselves,
giving his time,
yes, even his person,
to them.
    He knew perfectly well
    where this would lead him.
    He understood
    that it would lead to his death,
    to being killed,
    murdered on a cross.
    He even told them so.
It was Peter,
again Peter,
who spoke out,
and who said:
"Don't allow that,
don't be stupid,
don't be all good,
think of yourself,
forget about
those others,
don't exaggerate!"
    Jesus turned to Peter
    and said:
    "Get out of my way.
    Get away from me.
    Keep your mouth shut,
    you devil,
    you satan,
    get behind me!"
Don't you recognize the story?
Did it never happen to you
that you wanted to do some good
for someone:

to visit an old relation,
to comfort a sick person,
to adopt a lost child,
to send a nice card,
to give some alms,
to receive someone in your home,
to be kind to a refugee,
and that sometimes even those nearest to you,
members of your own family,
said:
"Don't do that;
don't make a fool of yourself.
In no time people will take advantage of you.
Don't be a friend to everyone.
Think of yourself,
think of us,
think of me!"
Did that never happen to you?
Of course it did.
Very often it did.
And did we always do
what Jesus did?
Did you,
or didn't you?
He asked us
to follow him,
to carry his cross,
to spread our arms
open,
as he did,
to those around us.

42.

RESPONSIBLE FOR EACH OTHER

Matthew 18:15–20

The gospel of today
is a very practical one.
It speaks about
our responsibility
for each other,
a responsibility
we all know of,
a responsibility
we often neglect.

     It was only a week ago
     that I met a friend of mine
     who asked me for prayers.
     I said,
     all right,
     but what am I supposed to pray for?
     It is always better to know.
     He told me,
     "Pray for me, my sister,
     and my father."

When I looked at him,
wondering what it was all about,
he added,
"My father is an old man.
My mother died some years ago;
my father is now very lonely,
and he started to do something he did before.
He started to drink heavily,
and now he has developed
a drinking problem,
a serious drinking problem.
But he does not want to admit it;
he says he has no drinking problem
because he never drinks during the day,
because he takes only a nightcap.
He says
that we exaggerate,
that he knows what he is doing
and things like that.

 Tomorrow the two of us,
 my sister and I,
 are going to speak with him,
 to tell him that he should stop,
 and, since we think
 that he will not be able to stop on his own,
 that he should ask for help;
 please pray for us."

Sisters and brothers,
it is about cases like this
that Jesus is speaking today.
It is for cases like this
that Jesus came into this world,
to ask us,
to plead with us,
to change our unhealthy ways.
He asks us
to be like him
in his relations with us,
in our relations with the ones around us, .

especially with those
who in one way or another depend
on us.
May I give you another example.
You know,
and most probably you know it better
than I do,
how so many marriages
end up in a kind of armistice,
a kind of armed and heavily guarded silence.

> The two,
> husband and wife,
> once lovers,
> once friends,
> once helping each other
> through the loneliness
> we all carry in ourselves,
> cannot speak with each other
> any more.
> The smallest thing
> is a source of endless irritation,
> a broken cup,
> a salty soup,
> a dent in the car,
> the choice of a TV program,
> the education of their children,
> though that is not a slight matter
> at all.
> Something went wrong,
> and often they don't know what.

What to do?
Sometimes the two ask for help.
Very rarely,
too rarely,
they will call in
—like Jesus suggests—
a third party,
a brother or a sister
or a friend.

In the heart of Africa,
where I have been for so long,
that third party
sits in the middle,
between them.
The husband sits on one side,
the wife sits on the other side.
And he would ask both of them:
"Tell me your story,
first you."
And she tells her story,
and when the husband tries to interrupt,
he would say:
"Keep quiet,
your turn will come.
Let her talk!"
Sometimes the husband says,
"Please, give me a piece of paper,
give me a pen.
I have to write that down,
I don't want to forget it,
I never thought about that!"
And then his turn comes,
and she has to listen.
Sometimes it is for the very first time
in their married lives
that they hear from each other
what they think,
telling their story
to that third one.
    After that,
    they often say:
    "Gosh,
    so that is what it was,
    that is what hindered us."
And the third one
says:
"Let us pray together."
And they pray together,

and just like Jesus foretold
and promised
in the gospel of today
that prayer
is
always
heard!

43.

BREAD AND ROSES

Matthew 18:21–35

We all know the scene.
We all have the same experience:
 "Please, forgive me,
 for this very last time.
 Please,
 it will never happen again,
 please, please . . . !!"
 But the car door closes,
 the train window remains empty,
 the plane flies off,
 the letter is never written,
 the telephone is put down,
 the debt is not forgiven,
 the gap remains,
 widening every day,
 wider and wider.
How often do you forgive
your brother?
How often do you forgive
your sister?

Peter asked for the limit.
Peter asked for the norm.
Though it was not really written down
the traditional Jewish answer was
four,
four times forgiveness,
and that is the end.
Peter suggested
seven,
seven times.
Peter thought himself to be
very generous.
We often use the limit of
three,
three times,
three warnings,
and then you go;
three warnings,
and that is the end;
three warnings,
and you have had it:
you lose your job,
your sustenance,
everything,
back on the street.
He broke through all that.
His answer
seven times seventy
does not mean
that we should not forgive
the four-hundred-and-ninety-first time.
It means
that we should forgive
always.
The reason is clear;
if we don't forgive,
our resentment
will be like a sediment,
dregs,

settling on the bottom
of the vessel of our lives,
    and slowly,
    slowly,
    our lives will be filled up,
    from the bottom to the top,
    from the beginning till the end,
    taking away all possibility
    to survive
    and celebrate.
We need forgiveness
like we need
bread and roses;
we need forgiveness
like we need air and water;
we need forgiveness
like we need a brother, and a sister,
a lover, and a friend.
    Not once,
    not twice,
    not thrice,
    not four times,
    not seven times,
    not seven times seventy times,
    but always.
    We do,
    we really do.

44.

HE SAID FRIEND

Matthew 20:1–16

How often do you forgive
your brother
was the question of last week.
How much do you pay
your sister
is the question of this week.
　　　Questions on human relations,
　　　questions on laws and regulations,
　　　questions of just and unjust,
　　　questions on rewards and fines,
　　　questions on right and wrong.
He tells us the story
about that landowner
and his workers,
those hired at midmorning,
those hired halfway through the day at noon,
those hired at four o'clock,
one hour before the day is over.
He tells how he paid them,
first those who had worked one hour,
then those who had worked for five hours,
then those who had worked for seven hours,

and finally those who had worked
the whole of the working day,
and how he paid them all the same!
 Of course,
 those last ones protested:
 this was impossible,
 had they not worked
 ten times as much!
 According to human practice,
 justice did not seem to have been done.
Wasn't it?
It was,
but in different way.
With one word,
Jesus changed the whole scene
in the story of today.
The landowner
does not treat his workers
as servants,
not even as brothers.
The landowner addresses them
in another way,
he calls them
friends.
 We are accustomed to calling each other
 sisters and brothers
 in Jesus' name.
 In Jesus' name,
 didn't he tell us
 that we all have one Father:
 our Father in heaven;
 and aren't we all formed
 from the same Mother:
 God's Earth?
 Aren't we descendants
 from the same ancestors:
 Adam and Eve?
Yet, he, Jesus himself,
hardly ever called us
brother or sister, .

only once, maybe.
He called us,
very explicitly:
friends.

You can have a brother
and not be his friend;
you can have a sister,
and not love her at all.
To be bloodrelated
is no guarantee
of love or respect.
The Bible is full
of that type of relationship:

Abel and Cain,
Isaac and Ishmael,
Jacob and Esau,
Joseph and his brothers.

It was not for nothing
that Peter had to ask
how often do I forgive
my *brother*?

He called us friends!
Of course, he is our brother,
but what is nicer
than to have your brother
as a friend;
than to be the friend
of your sister?

It is that relation
that changes all,
even in the story of today!
*What a friend
we have in Jesus*!
And for the rest,
aren't we all workers,
who started
at that very last hour?

45.

VISION AND LAW

Matthew 21:28–32

Again and again
they came to him
to say:
"Listen,
why is it
that you are not faithful to the law
like we are;
that you don't obey
as we obey;
that you don't pay your dues
as we pay;
that you do not fast
as we fast;
that you don't even respect
the most sacred of all laws,
and that you dare to heal on sabbath days?
     And nevertheless,
     you say
     that God is your Father,
     that you have access to Him,
     that you are God's Son,

and you even seem to work miracles
in God's name.
How come?"
He answered them
with his parable about those two sons:
the one who said *yes*,
and did *no*;
and the one who said *no*,
and did *yes*.

His answer was subtle.
He did not say
that those who obey all
God's laws and regulations
are not going to heaven;
they will
and they do.
He did not say
that tax-collectors and prostitutes
who don't follow
those laws and regulations,
do the will of God;
they don't.
What he said was
that those sinners
believe faster
than those who were caught
in their conformity
to all those laws.

What he said was
that those tax-collectors and prostitutes
were more open
to the new vision
than those who thought
they had seen,
counted,
and computed
it all.
It is according to him
not only a question of laws,

authority, and obedience.
It is a question of vision,
intuition, and faith,
too.

>Law-abiding church people
>are facing
>this very same issue
>again and again.

When we meet a person
who is different from us,
who does not seem to stick to the law
as we do,
who eats,
who drinks,
and seems to live frivolously and lightheartedly,
who is totally free,
and who, nevertheless, speaks of God,
in a word,
when we meet someone
who seems to be
like Jesus
was,
we are facing
the same dilemma.

>We can be so trapped
>in knowing exactly
>what we should do,
>and what should be done,
>in view of the laws
>made in God's name
>that we can be caught in a framework
>that does not allow us to see
>any further than that.

We should not be sinners,
oh no;
but we should not be trapped
either.
We should be able to see!

46.

THE EARTH IS OURS

Matthew 21:33–43

He was a young refugee,
standing in front of me.
He had black blazing eyes,
he looked very thin and wiry,
he told me about his hunger,
he told me about his country,
he asked me for help,
a help I could not give
at the moment he asked.
> He asked for a piece of bread.
> I gave him a piece,
> it was not much
> but I hadn't any more.
> Suddenly he got very excited,
> he bent down over the earth,
> and hitting the ground
> with both his fists,
> he said:
> "This earth is not yours,
> this earth is not mine,
> this earth is God's,
> this earth is ours.

Your food is not yours,
your food is not mine,
all food is God's,
all food is ours."
And he repeated:
"Not yours,
not mine,
but God's,
ours!"
And then he said,
with a softness in his eyes
that I had not seen in them before:
"You know,
I am Jesus,
I came
back to this world,"
and wrapping the piece of bread
I had given him
in some brown paper,
he left,
greeting me from the corner of the street
with a wave of his arm.
    I thought:
    "The hunger got into
    his head."
    Hadn't it?
We, in the West,
or in the North,
if you prefer that,
live in the best vineyard of the Lord.
All goes well,
rain in time,
plenty of sun,
excellent seed,
beautiful growth,
corn-fed cattle,
plenty of beef,
very rich milk,
much too much butter. .

All sheds and barns,
all warehouses and silos,
are more than full
with enough for years and years.
And what we don't grow here,
but like to eat,
we import from the East,
or from the South,
if you prefer that.

> And now, there are those people
> at our doors
> from that East and that South,
> hungry and miserable,
> poor and wretched,
> asking for their share.

Are they his servants,
the ones
of the parable of today?
Or, maybe,
maybe,
are they
HE, himself,
in all of them?

47.

INVITED TOGETHER

Matthew 22:1–14

It had been God's intention,
from the very beginning,
to bring them all together
in the end,
gathering them
from all over the earth,
in their parental home.
    A dream maintained,
    in spite of the news
        about Abel and Cain,
        Noah and his sons,
        Babel and its tower,
        Isaac and Ishmael,
        Jacob and Esau,
        Joseph and his brothers,
        the Jews and Pharaoh,
        World War I and World War II,
        the holocaust and apartheid.
Hadn't God given
each of them
his genius,

or her talent?
Hadn't God given
each of them
part of the human inheritance?
> It is a dream
> so often expressed
> by God's prophets
> who sowed the seed
> of this dream and this vision
> indelibly
> in the hearts and minds
> of all those faithful
> to God's will.

Isaiah foretold
how one day all nations
would come together,
climbing the mountain of the Lord;
coming together to share and celebrate;
tearing away all veils
that hide us from each other;
tearing the webs
that keep us apart;
drying all tears
that were ever shed;
removing all differences and discriminations;
bringing them together
to a banquet,
a feast of rich food and choice wines.
> Jesus told them then,
> and he is telling us now:
> "It is time,
> the food is prepared,
> the bullocks and the corn-fed cattle
> are killed,
> everything is ready,
> come to the feast!"

But we say:
"Not yet,
we are not yet ready. .

I have to tend *my* farm,
I have to look after *my* business,
I have no time to socialize with others,
I am not willing to share,
I am not prepared to let go,
I am not going to come,
I am certainly not,
I am not going to sit down with all those strangers."
And we laugh at those among us
who say
that we can't go on living
    as we are doing:
    acting as if
    we don't belong together at all;
    acting as if
    we have nothing in common,
    neither God our Father,
    nor the earth our Mother;
    acting as if
    there are walls between us,
    the blacks and the whites,
    the young and the old,
    the rich and the poor,
    men and women.
    Discrimination and apartheid
    everywhere.
He told us
the whole story.
I don't know
at what stage of the story
we are now.
I do know
that the meal is ready,
I do know
where we will be
when we do not accept his invitation
to be together,
or not to be
at all.

48.

TRANSCENDING THEM

Matthew 22:15–21

They came to him that day
not to ask a question;
they came to him
to trap him.
They wanted to draw their nets
around him,
so that he would not be able to escape from them
anymore.
> They failed.
> He won,
> but he knew
> that in the end
> he would lose.
They had been consulting each other,
they had weighed his possible answers,
they had constructed an inescapable dilemma,
that is what they thought.
They wanted him to choose
between his people
and its oppressors,
between the Jews
and the Romans.

And whatever choice he made,
he would be caught.
Choosing the Romans
would mean being rejected by most of the Jews;
choosing his people,
he would be arrested by the Romans.
　　　They came to him
　　　to trap him;
　　　notwithstanding their beautiful pious faces,
　　　their hearts were filled
　　　with bad faith.
They said:
"Teacher,
we are facing a problem,
and would like your advice.
Should we pay tax to the Romans,
or shouldn't we?"
　　　He looked at them
　　　while they were speaking.
　　　People started to surround them,
　　　hearing the question,
　　　understanding the trap,
　　　eager to hear
　　　what he would say.
They did not have to wait too long
for his answer.
It came like a flash.
"Show me a coin,"
he told them,
and they showed him a coin,
a Roman coin
that they had already bought
for payment of their taxes.
He looked at it
and asked,
showing them the head,
"Whose face is that?"
They answered:
"Caesar's,".

and he said:
"Give to Caesar,
what is Caesar's,"
and he added:
"And to God,
what is God's!"
>He escaped
>from their dilemma
>by referring to a reality
>that transcended
>the difference
>they had wanted to make.
His interest was not the Jews,
his interest was not the Romans,
his interest was not only one group,
his interest was the Kingdom of God,
a Kingdom comprising the whole of the human family,
pagan and Jew,
Jacob and Cyrus,
alike.
>He escaped their dilemma,
>and made his choice clear.
>He was not willing to play
>Romans against Jews,
>or Jews against Romans.
>He opted for another world
>where those divisions,
>where fascist *apartheid*,
>would not exist anymore.
>They got the point,
>*and they rejected it completely.*
>That is why he won,
>but also lost.
>He escaped this time,
>but his battle was lost
>in this world.
>Opting for God,
>and God's Kingdom,

the whole family of humanity,
it was only God
who would be able
to save him.
And that is what God did.

49.

OUR NEIGHBOR NOWADAYS

Matthew 22:34–40

It was a hot afternoon in Thika,
a small Kenyan town.
School children were going home,
playing as children do.
Some girls were throwing
a ball
made of some old papers
kept together by an old rubber band.
They were playing alongside
the barbed wire fence
of the enormous pineapple plantation
owned by one of the largest transnational fruit companies
in the world.
As far as you could see,
those purplish fruits
were coloring the hillsides.
The girls did not look;
they were accustomed to the sight,
and they had heard too many sighs of their parents
because of those fruits;
they were playing with their ball.

Suddenly an unexpected gust of wind blew
the ball under the wire fence.
    Just at that moment
    some of the plantation guards
    with their fierce dogs
    came from behind a bush.
    They saw the girls
    creeping under the fence
    to get their ball.
    They let loose their dogs
    who attacked the girls.
    Shouts of fear and anguish.
    The dogs were called back.
    They came, reluctantly,
    licking their mouths with rosy tongues.
One girl,
let us call her Jane,
Jane Wanjiku wa Chege,
a beautiful one,
her family's hope,
thirteen years old,
was bleeding to death;
another one
kept her mauled face in her hands.
    That night the usual goods-train
    left Thika's railway station
    with its freight of goods,
    canned pineapple,
    for the European market.
    One of the canners
    was Chege,
    the father of Jane Wanjiku,
    who was working as a day worker,
    just as 9000 out of the 10,000 other
    fruit canners and plantation workers in Thika
    do.
    In that way the company
    can go under
    .the minimun national monthly salary,

remaining without further social obligations,
too.
It keeps the prices
in our world very low,
and in their world,
extremely high.
Some weeks later,
there was a party,
a birthday party somewhere in Europe.
A girl,
why shouldn't we call her Jane, too,
was turning thirteen,
a beautiful girl,
the pride of her family.
She had been allowed to choose
what to eat as dessert at the party,
and she had chosen
pineapple with whipped cream.

>Before they started to eat,
>Jane asked the guests to pray,
>and she prayed,
>"*O, almighty God,*
>*who in your goodness*
>*gave us all this food,*
>*and especially these fruits,*
>*as a sign of your goodness,*
>*we thank you for your bounty.*
>*Amen.*"

The prayer was not heard
in Thika,
maybe that's a good thing,
but it should have been heard,
nevertheless,
just like the story of Jane Wanjiku wa Chege,
should have been told
to the celebrating Jane.

>One day it may be widely told,
>today it was told here,
>all of you heard it.

And even this is not the full story.
Do you know
why they grow pineapples for us
in that African land
that hardly can feed itself?
Because that gigantic fruit company got into trouble
with trade union tendencies in the Philippines,
and they had come to the Philippines
because they had got into the same trouble before in Hawaii,
and even before that
in the United States.
There is no doubt
about that. . . .
     Do you see
     how we hang together?
     Do you see
     who your neighbor is,
     in this, our world?
     Do you understand the impact
     of the words of Jesus,
     the man who saw all this
     in his divine-human heart,
     so long before anyone else?
Love your neighbor!
But who is my neighbor?
Love your neighbor
like you love yourself,
in the name of God,
who loves us all!

50.

WHERE ARE YOU FROM?

Matthew 23:3–12

It was in the dark of night,
in the dark of the darkest night,
about two thousand years ago,
that a remark was made
that had been made so often before;
that is still made
innumerable times every day;
and that should never be made anymore,
with Him
among us.

     It was a harassing scene.
     Jesus had been arrested.
     He was standing in front of a set of his judges.
     Outside,
     in the dark,
     it was cold,
     very cold.
     People were sitting around a fire,
     with their hands outstretched
     in the fleeting warmth of the flames.
It was then
that a busy maid,

selling her wares,
pointed at Peter and said:"
"Your accent betrays you,
where are you from?"

> She tried to classify him,
> she tried to localize him,
> she tried to place him,
> she tried to catch him
> and to pin him down,
> in his descent,
>> his blood,
>> his land,
>> his tribe,
>> and his nation.

Peter denied
knowing Jesus;
he denied the truth;
Peter should have denied
something else:
he should have denied,
that he was any longer
classifiable as a Galilean,
as belonging to one group,
> to one land,
> and to one nation.

That is what the gospel of today is about.
"Do not call anyone on earth
your father!"
Do not use any classification
by descent,
by blood,
by land,
by tribe,
by nation
anymore.
That time
is over.
Those divisions
are gone.

From now on it is
all of us,
one descent,
one blood,
one land,
one people,
and one nation.
"Only one is your father,
the one in heaven!"
Only one is your mother,
the Earth,
God's womb,
from which the Father begot us.

How often did it not happen to me,
how often did it not happen to you,
in whatever region or country you were,
that people said
what that maid said
so long ago,
in the dark of the night,
the darkest of all nights:
"Your accent betrays you,
where are you from?"
Where am I from?
Where are you from?
Where are the others from?
The answer Jesus gave
is for all of us:

"Only one is your father,
the one in heaven!"
You belong together,
you are brothers and sisters,
you should be friends.
It is only
when this answer will be given
by all
to that *treacherous* question
that we will be at home
together,

here on Earth,
and in all time
to come.
    It is only this answer
    that can break the dark of the night
    in which we are still sitting in this world,
    with our hands outstretched
    in the fleeting warmth
    of some fire.

51.

THAT MIDNIGHT CRY

Matthew 22:34–40

The headline read:
"BRILLIANT STUDENT ENDS LIFE."
Another one
slipped away
from us,
    from us:
    aren't we all together in this?
He shot himself,
seventeen years old,
before anyone could rescue him
from the room in which he had locked
himself.
    Not the first one,
    not the last one either.
He was young, brilliant,
humorous, ebullient,
cooperative, and fine,
a school representative,
and considering the large number of students
who came to the funeral,
a very good friend.

> There were plenty of flowers,
> beautiful ones,
> in all kinds of colors,
> sad gestures and symbols,
> expressing the powerlessness and grief
> of those who gave them
> after his death.

The Reverend who led the service
did not know what to say,
so he said,
"It all seems to be so meaningless,"
and saying this
he indicated
the sense of it all.
Isn't that where the danger lies,
especially when you are young,
a virgin in life
without too many bonds
to keep you?

> The meaninglessness,
> the lack of point,
> the lack of pith,
> the lack of aim,
> the lack of purpose,
> the lack of a sense
> of being taken up in something,
> the stressing of the trivia of life
> all the time,
> all the time,
> day and night,
> all the time. . . .

Many of us are waiting
for something to happen;
many of us are waiting
for someone to arrive;
we are all on edge:
the young ones
more
than the older ones;.

the virgins
more
than those initiated.
>The new ones
>need a greater hope,
>more hope,
>to avoid,
>and to escape from,
>mere fate.
In Jesus' parable of today
the virgins are waiting
for the coming of their Lord,
for the beginning of the banquet.
>Some waited
>wisely,
>with all the substance they needed
>to feed their fire
>and their light.
>Others waited
>foolishly,
>without the substance they needed
>to feed that fire
>and that light.
Yet, they were all waiting,
the wise and the foolish;
they knew something
was going to happen,
though they fell asleep.
>I wonder whether this story
>applies to us.
>Are we really waiting
>for a Lord to come;
>are we really waiting
>for a banquet to start;
>are we really organizing
>our lives
>in view of that change
>at the end of time?

Are we trimming our lamps,
feeding the flames,
in view of Kingdom to come?
No wonder
that some of us
give up,
the young ones
first. . . .
It seems to be dark,
dark all around us,
everyone is asleep,
all have forgotten.
MIDNIGHT.
It is time
for someone to shout again
that midnight cry
at this very hour:
"*The groom is coming,
let us get up to greet him!*"

52.   .

MINISTERING MONEY

Matthew 25:14–30

After their grand pastoral on peace,
the American bishops
wrote a letter on money,
on capital and the economy.
> They wrote
> that in the actual situation
> society is so complicated
> that Christians hardly ever manage to see
> how things hang together,
> how the economy and their spiritual life
> have anything to do with each other.
> Money seems to be
> a spiritual embarrassment,
> just like their bodies are
> to so very many.
Jesus does not suffer from this scrupulosity.
He often speaks about money
and about the economy.
He does it in the gospel of today,
in a story
he repeated very often,

in one form
or another.
>It is the story
>about him
>leaving for a journey.
>It is the story
>about him
>coming back from that journey.
>It is the story
>about us
>being charged with the running of the household,
>in his absence;
>it is the story
>about us
>being charged with the running of his vineyard
>while he is away.
It is a tale
about tasks
to be fulfilled,
about talents
to be used,
about money
to be invested.
It is the story
about the Kingdom
to be realized.
>How could he not have spoken
>about money,
>while making it
>was such a clear possibility
>for him?
>Wasn't it his first temptation?
>Didn't the devil ask him
>to change stones into bread,
>and is bread not the ultimate
>gold?
In principle his solution
is simple.

We should use all we are
and all we have
in view of the Kingdom.
In practice his solution
causes problems:
how do you invest
in his Kingdom?

    Jesus speaks in these parables
    about those who are afraid,
    about those who are lazy,
    who do not use their talents,
    and who hide their money away.
    He blames them:
    they should invest,
    work,
    and participate.

There is another group of people
who do not participate
for another reason:
the ones who are so poor and miserable
that they need all their efforts
to be able to survive,
and who never ever
are capable of being themselves,
uncovering their talents.
They, too, are
treasures that remain hidden,
pearls that will not be found,
fish remaining in the deep of the sea,
light that never shines.

    He himself
    used all his power
    and all his expertise
    to bring people out,
    to bring them to themselves,
    to liberate them,
    to convince the poor and the lowly
    that they have content and worth,

that they should come out of their hiding,
and participate.
He opted
—as one says
nowadays—
for the poor
and the wretched.
It is in that way
that our money, our talents and our time
should be invested,
not in charity and food alone
        —that kind of help
        neither touches the heart of your business,
        nor the crux of his—
but on a development program
that engages
those who are left out
in the society we are building,
so that all may be taken up
in that growing network
among us,
the network of God,
his Kingdom.

53.

THE INHERITORS
OF THE KINGDOM

Matthew 25:31–46

When we think of a king,
we imagine him
sitting on a throne,
higher than all the others,
with his subjects
in front of him,
bending low,
walking on their tiptoes,
and speaking in very low voices,
not daring to laugh,
or to shout,
because in the presence of that king,
they feel not to be kings at all.
>   We think of someone
>   who has a large army,
>   with swords and horses,
>   with guns and planes,
>   who goes to battle
>   against all those
>   who do not belong to his kingdom,

and who by that mere fact,
are his enemies.
Enemies,
he has to fight.
When we celebrated
the feast of Christ the King
in the past,
we often celebrated it
as if he was such a king.
I remember
how as a child
we marched in a long parade
to the main square of my native town.
There Christ was sitting,
our King,
high on a throne,
a statue in stone
with a heart of real gold.
And we were standing there,
singing very martial hymns,
and we pledged our fidelity
to Christ,
our King,
and we shouted with loud voices
that we were willing
to fight his enemies.
We even knew exactly
who his enemies were,
the unconverted,
the non-Christians,
the Nazis,
the Communists,
but also the man
down the street
who did not go to Sunday Mass
anymore.
Reading the gospel of today,
we know, of course,
that we were wrong.

That gospel
does not speak about Christ
being our king
in that way.
It speaks about Jesus.
It tells how
Jesus
is sitting on a throne,
that is true;
but sitting on that throne,
he does not reserve his kingship
to himself alone.
He tells us
that we can be kings and queens,
like he.

He says:
"If you feed the hungry,
if you give water to the thirsty,
if you dress the naked,
if you comfort the sick,
if you visit the prisoners,
if you welcome the stranger,
you belong to the kingdom,
you will inherit the kingdom."
And aren't those
who
inherit a kingdom
queens and kings,
too?

If you take this,
his norm,
if you believe
his judgment,
then his kingdom
and its inheritance
cannot be restricted
to us alone.
It does not run
according to ideological,

geographical,
political,
or religious
borders and lines.
It is a reality
that breaks through all that.
    A Catholic is a king
    when he feeds the hungry,
    but a Hindu is, too.
An American is a queen
when she gives water to the thirsty,
but so is a Russian.
    A liberal is a king
    when he visits a prisoner,
    but a conservative who visits a prisoner
    is one also.
A democrat is a queen
when she comforts the sick,
just as well as a republican who does the same.
    You are like Jesus
    when you receive a stranger as a guest,
    but your child
    who does the same
    is of the same royal stock
    as you.
In this way,
Jesus' Kingdom,
—but shouldn't we prefer to call it
the Kingdom of Christ—
is a reign and a *network*
that extends through
all the world,
from the East to the West,
from the North to the South.
    A kingdom still hidden,
    but revealing itself,
    more and more,
    forming
    Christ's Body
    itself.

INDEX OF SCRIPTURAL TEXTS

Matthew

1:18-24	*20*
2:1-12	*34*
3:1-12	*9*
4:1-11	*68*
4:12-23	*42*
5:1-11	*45*
5:13-16	*50*
5:17-37	*54*
5:38-48	*58*
6:24-34	*61*
7:21-27	*65*
11:2-11	*14*
11:25-30	*137*
13:1-23	*141*
13:24-43	*145*
13:44-52	*149*
14:13-21	*153*
14:22-33	*157*
15:21-28	*161*
16:13-19	*133*
16:13-20	*166*
16:21-27	*170*
17:1-9	*72*
18:15-20	*174*
18:21-35	*179*
20:1-16	*182*
21:28-32	*185*

21:33-43	*188*
22:1-14	*191*
22:15-21	*194*
22:34-40	*198, 206*
23:3-12	*202*
24:37-44	*5*
25:14-30	*210*
25:31-46	*214*
26:14-27:66	*89*

Luke

2:15-20	*26*
2:16-21	*29*
24:13-35	*100*

John

1:29-34	*37*
3:16-18	*125*
4:5-42	*76*
6:51-58	*130*
9:1-14	*80*
10:1-10	*104*
11:1-45	*85*
14:1-12	*107*
14:15-21	*111*
17:1-11	*115*
20:1-9	*92*
20:19-23	*120*
20:19-31	*96*